Demons in My Marriage Bed

A True Story of Spiritual Warfare

Paul Villanueva, M.A.

Linda Villanueva, B.S.

ISBN 978-1-942019-02-2 (Paperback)

ISBN 978-0-983764-44-1 (eBook)

Table of Contents

Printed Edition Notes by the Publisher

Three years ago in 2011, the eBook version of this book was published, and since that time, many testified the book was indeed a help and fortification for them. It has helped both individuals and couples learn about the spiritual forces behind their problems and complexities. The eBook especially assisted those who were experiencing a severe personal haunting by demonic spirits. Although many were moved by the authors' transparent and candid story of their personal haunting, they were even more inspired by the tools, training, and resources given to fight these demons in their own lives.

The past three years have been a proving ground for what is written in this book, and the authors would not change or retract one single word from this effective work. Using the strategies and tactics outlined in their own book, they have gone on to fight many more spiritual battles, and overcoming always through the power and authority which God gives.

In this printed edition, the entire original text is included along with a chapter dedicated to using the technique of self-deliverance from demons to set any sincere reader free from the torments of evil. Additionally, material has been added to bring the reader up to date regarding the authors' ministry as a result of their publishing the first eBook edition. Those who wish to study further and go deeper into other works by the authors are encouraged to read the added material outlining the contents of their current books on spiritual warfare, the church, Gnosticism, and Christian living.

Chapter 1: The Martial Marriage

Blessed be the LORD, my rock, who trains my hands for war, and my fingers for battle (Psalm 144:1).

Let us get down to business. We will make it direct, and powerful - like a boxer's jab to the jaw. This book is about engaging in spiritual warfare in marriage. It is about making the correct choices to live your life in freedom and in power. No person alone can defeat Satan or his demonic deceptions. Only through the authority of Christ Jesus will you ever overcome the deception, torture, and eventual destruction of your marriage by demonic forces.

This book is about our true story - a frightening story of witchcraft, demonic control, spell casting, strange occurrences, tormenting fear, and finally redemption. It is a story of adultery co-mingled with the darkest satanic deceptions we ever experienced. It is out of this life and death struggle that we learned the art of having a Martial Marriage. We learned to fight on a spiritual level, things, which were manifesting in the natural realm.

The ability to overcome can only be accomplished through the power of God's Spirit working in your marriage. You or your partner (ideally both) must believe that God became man, died for your sins, was buried, and rose from the dead to cleanse you and give you eternal life. You must receive this free gift of salvation through Christ Jesus before you can incorporate the techniques in this book. All guidance is based on Scripture. So if you do not believe in the Lord Jesus for salvation with belief in God's Word contained in the Bible, you will get nothing from this work. From here forward, we write to the "believer."

We use the term, "Martial Marriage" as it relates to the term "Martial Arts." Just as one may train in fighting and warfare techniques, the "Martial Marriage" is a marriage trained and disciplined in the art of spiritual warfare. Training for a Martial Marriage consists of you and your spouse understanding your enemy and living the Scriptures to effectively combat his deceit. This is no easy task. If you and your spouse are Christ followers and have made a commitment to live for God, you and your marriage will be under attack in one form or another at opportune times.

What about the joy Christ brings? What about the blessings and love? Yes, that will be there, but so will the constant threat of Satan trying to steal it from you. Learning to fight is essential. Satan is not equal to God. This is not a fight between good and evil, or light and darkness as if they were co-equal in power. It is important to realize that Satan has already been defeated. God is all-powerful and your enemy is not. However, because of our ignorance in what the Scriptures say about our enemy and his tactics, coupled with our ignorance regarding God's redemptive work for us, we often succumb to Satan's traps and destruction.

Additionally, at times, we bring curses on ourselves through disobedience and rebellion to God, thus we open the door to demonic attacks. Other times God allows demonic attacks to bring spiritual growth and faith building in our lives as we walk in the Spirit in the sanctification or holiness process. Understanding this is crucial. Remember, nothing can happen to you unless God allows it. You and your spouse must become a team, an elite fighting unit, trained in the art of spiritual warfare. This is not an independent military action by only one spouse. It will not work like that. Both of you must be joined together, train together, and fight together.

No elite team, whether it is a police S.W.A.T. team, the Navy Seals, the Army Rangers, or the Green Berets accomplish their mission independently. They operate as a unit, each person having a specified job and action. Egos and jealousy have no place with an elite fighting team. If a S.W.A.T. member is assigned to move forward into a dangerous situation, they count on other members to guard the sides and the rear. Imagine if one team member decided to not participate because he felt lazy, rejected, or tired? Some other member may be killed. IMPORTANT: Both spouses must eventually commit to doing spiritual warfare in their marriage, or else the one slacking leaves the other open to attack and destruction. Weakness is unacceptable. Period.

Weakness refers to a spouse that professes to be a Christian, but fails to train hard. When in the heat of battle, the weak one will cower and retreat leaving the strong one to fight alone. Weakness is not newness. A rookie is tolerated and trained by his superiors, but not allowed to engage in high-risk scenarios until they have learned the rules of engagement. Weakness is "knowing better," but failing to support the other spouse and failing to totally commit and submit to the authority of God. Men are weak when they refuse to accept the God-given responsibility of being the priest over their family and offering spiritual protection. They are weak men if they allow their wives to assume the role of priest. Women are weak when they fail to respect their husband's priestly role and submit under his spiritual guidance and protection. It takes a team to train and fight together in a Martial Marriage.

Why is marriage important to God? The marriage union contains "mysteries" of Heaven. The Apostle Paul wrote to the church in Ephesus stating, "Wives submit to your own husband . . . the husband is head as Christ is head of the church . . . the church is subject to Christ . . . husbands love your wives as Christ loved the church . . . we are members of Christ's body, of His flesh and bones . . . a man shall be joined to his wife and the two shall become one . . . this is a great mystery concerning Christ and the church."

Marriage is not an "agreement" but a "covenant" with another person. A covenant cannot be broken as an agreement can. God entered into a covenant relationship with His people and so marriage mirrors that relationship of faithfulness, trust, love, discipline, and protection. Our marriages reflect the character of God!

God said, "And this is the second thing you do: You cover the altar of the LORD with tears, with weeping and crying; so He does not regard the offering anymore, nor receive it with goodwill from your hands. Yet you say, for what reason? Because the LORD has been witness between you and the wife of your youth, with whom you have dealt treacherously; yet she is your companion and your wife by covenant . . ." (Malachi 2:13,14).

Clear enough? Read it again if there is any doubt. In a very real sense, your spouse is your first line of defense. Your spouse is the one who holds you accountable, ministers to you, and is your ultimate brother or sister in Christ. When you get angry, lustful, hateful, prideful, or vengeful, it is not your pastor who holds you accountable, as they are not living with you. It will be your spouse who first notices something wrong in your attitude or behavior. It will be your spouse who prays or gives a Word from God. And if you produce children, then these Godly attributes will be passed onto them so they will not depart from the learning of God.

This is not a psychology book. It will not give you counseling techniques to make your marriage warm and fuzzy, or nice and cozy. If you want to read about what psychologists think about your problems then put this book down now and walk away, it is not for you. This book is about sin and repentance – love and war. It is about being broken before God so He can use you in

His kingdom. It is like a punch in the face. It will get your attention. It is about what your enemy, Satan, desires to do to you. He will do it if you and your spouse do not understand the concept of having a Martial Marriage.

These spiritual fighting techniques are for protection against a stronger, smarter, larger, and more experienced opponent. He is much bigger than you are without Christ. Learning to fight for your life and engaging in spiritual warfare is not an option - it is a must. Developing a Martial Marriage means submitting to God, and building a relationship with Him. He covers you like a helmet, shield, and ballistic vest covers a military soldier. However, you still must put on the protection. You and your spouse still must use and train in the defenses and weaponry provided for you.

This is not a book about "works," and impressing God with religious activities. Rather it is a book about training, practicing, and fighting for the sanctification that is yours. It is about pressing hard into the Kingdom of Heaven. This is no daisy stroll, and certainly not for the weak in spirit. This book is Bible based. It will offend some people. Others will dismiss it as nonsense and paranoia. Some will get angry. That is fine. Some readers will be convicted by the Holy Spirit to repent of sin, turn to Jesus, and receive Him as Lord of their entire lives and marriages. Some readers will be called to a deeper understanding and relationship with God the Father.

This book is not about Satan and his demons, but points to Christ and His redemption. If you are tired of living a mediocre life or a tormented one, then get angry with your enemy. Satan is out to kill you and your family. Get furious. Becoming a warrior is a process, which takes real life experience, real life combat. We have that combat experience, and that is why we write with so much confidence. Read on and get ready to rumble, but this is not a sport match, rather a fight to the death.

The War Zone

There was an intense heavenly battle for Paul's soul. This experience took us on a journey that changed our lives forever – a journey we must share as a warning to others. We came very close to losing our marriage and possibly our very lives. Paul is a different man from the one that was – now renewed in mind and in spirit. Dead is the old man, stripped of self-strength, ego, perversion, and arrogance. He lies at the foot of the cross, and worships the only true almighty God of creation. He is a new man, one filled with the Holy Spirit and full of faith.

But, victory did not come without a fight, and even with victory, other skirmishes constantly beckon us to engage in battle. The war rages on because we enlisted in the spiritual battle when we believed on the Lord Jesus Christ for salvation. We do not want anyone to think that this book is the end of our story, and now life is as if it was before but with peace, joy, and love. Our lives have changed, and will not ever be the same.

We rest in God, but are constantly alert to the dangers of the enemy. We become smaller and smaller and yield to Christ, so that he can become larger and larger in us. We now learn new fighting techniques to resist the enemy, and we learn of his strategies to destroy us. We are in a continual war zone. Living in holiness before our magnificent God is the only way we can survive.

Christ said He came to destroy the works of Satan. So, through Him we are His wrecking machines. It is a fact that we fought real demons. We battled real witchcraft and the occult. We were the victims of satanic rituals, and were under very real demonic spells. However, this story does not focus on the supernatural, but on redemption. It is focused on Jesus. It points only to Christ. It is a true story – every word of it. Nothing embellished. No literary license was used. The goal is to warn others of the very real demonic forces, which desire to destroy every Christian life and marriage, and to point the way to the only saving grace of Jesus Christ.

What gives us credibility? Our scars give us credibility. We have the scars of Christ. As we live for and in Him, we have been refined, purged, and put through the fire for His purpose. We are continually being tested, tried, and pushed to obtain higher levels of communion with our God. We bear the marks of our sins and mistakes. We live with the consequences of our actions. We are battle tested, but do not claim to be perfect.

For example, suppose you were being trained to be a soldier in the military. One of your instructors teaching you about the enemy forces, and instructing you on combat tactics is a graduate from the finest military academy, has a degree from college, has studied war intellectually, and yet has never been in a real fight. Your other instructor is not intellectual, has no degree, and has not associated with a military academy, but has real life combat experience. This instructor has survived the heat of the battle and knows from experience what works and what does not work. Whom do you want to train with? What instructor should teach you? I will tell you right now that I would take the instructor with real life experience over the book-learned intellectual any day.

The writers of the Bible wrote from experience and Holy Spirit inspiration. They did not approach their writing from a purely analytical or intellectual point of view. Because of their experience, we can be confident in the Scriptures that give us techniques, and tactics for defeating the enemy of our lives and marriages. For example, when the Apostle James writes, "Submit yourself to God, then resist the devil, and then he will run from you," (James 4:7), he is giving us a battle tactic for survival based on his experience in spiritual combat.

So realize that you and your spouse are in a war zone, realize that you need to use spiritual weapons against the enemy, and realize you must put on the whole armor of God so that you can stand against the enemy's attack.

You can only do this if you are a Christ follower. If you are not a Christ follower, and do not believe on Jesus Christ for your salvation, then you are lost, and on your own with the certainty of defeat and destruction. You and your spouse must first repent of all sin, receive Jesus Christ into your hearts and commit to being renewed in Him before any of the techniques in this book will work.

Chapter 2: Sex, Satan, and Salvation

" . . . For perhaps he departed for a while for this purpose, that you might receive him forever."
(Philemon 1:15)

In the Apostle Paul's letter to Philemon, he writes about Philemon's run-away slave who heard and believed in the Gospel of Christ. Paul urged Philemon to take Onesimus back, not as a slave, but as a brother in Christ. Perhaps Onesimus ran away so that he could return and be with Philemon forever in his new role of "brother."

I (Paul) am a real life Onesimus. I am that bondservant of God who ran away from Him. For a while I was missing, running, rebelling, and being disobedient. Then because of the extreme torment and suffering I caused in my life, I found my way back to God and returned to Him forever, not as a slave, but as a son. Maybe the reason I was allowed to run away was so that I could return. It is obvious that had I not hit rock bottom with the demonic tormentors tearing at my very soul, I would have not been driven into the arms of God and His Christ.

Before running away, I had a very real encounter with Christ Jesus as a teenager, but allowed myself to slowly slip away from fellowship with God over the years. My slip started with sexual sin. I had sex with a girlfriend about three years after my conversion. I never repented of this sexual sin or any other subsequent sexual sins. I simply justified my actions because I was a young man. I thought having multiple sex partners was just what young men do.

As an adult, even though I called myself a "Christian," I had a form of spirituality, but was far removed from Biblical truth. In fact, I was deep into occult practices, and did not even realize the extent of my rituals and beliefs, which took me into the realms of darkness.

New Age Wisdom

My occult spirituality began in my late thirties with several factors leading me into the desire for supernatural power. One of the events occurred when we moved onto a ranch nestled in ancient Native American territory. There were ancient petro-glyphs and artifacts near us. I began to have a strong fascination with Indian rituals, herbal medicines, spiritual beliefs, and magic. Many New Age philosophies and teachers have hijacked the true historical Native American culture. These New Age masters sell their ancient nature worship in the guise of Native American practices. It was this New Age philosophy that I bought into.

During this period, I began to dream significant dreams and obtained the ability to interpret them for others. Many people contacted me on a regular basis for dream interpretation. Keeping a "book of dreams," I would journal each significant vision I had, which some had real prophetic fulfillments. One night, I had a vision dream that these men were standing around me while I slept in bed. They spoke an unknown language, but I knew they were Native American. Although they spoke an ancient dialect, I understood what they were saying. One asked the other, "Should we give him the gift?" I always thought the "gift" was the ability to interpret dreams for others, as I could not interpret the meanings of my own dreams.

I studied spirit animals for myself and for others. I had two; the red tailed hawk and the diamond back rattlesnake. Several rattlesnakes had "given up their lives" to me, and I had their rattles in my shaman box with feathers, white sage, tobacco, and other fetishes. At one point, I brought a rattlesnake head to work with me and kept it on my desk to ward off my enemies. It was placed next to my small statue of a coiled rattler. Additionally, I used the movements of a coiled snake and its strike in some of my martial arts practices. Also, I used the grace and power combination of the red tailed hawk in striking my opponents.

Not only were snake and hawk my brothers, I obtained great "owl magic" from the barn owls, which nested above my head in the outside crevice created between the house eaves and the patio cover. I believed this owl magic gave me the ability to see into difficult situations, and understand systems, and philosophies.

A "medicine bundle" was always in my pocket or in my briefcase nearby during critical times like promotional interviews. If I found myself in a hard situation with another person, I would secretly hold onto the bundle hidden within my pocket. I believed it gave me power.

It contained dirt from my father's grave, a Masonic square and compass pin, a coyote tooth and some white sage.

I only purchased and read two types of books, those written about Native American practices and those written about the ancient Chinese culture. My bookshelves were lined with New Age knowledge and dozens of martial arts fighting techniques, as well as, esoteric Chinese knowledge of breathing and meditation exercises. I also collected dozens of videotapes and DVDs relating to the same themes.

The ancient Chinese culture mesmerized me because I was studying the martial arts. This was the second occurrence that influenced me into the occult. I had earned a second-degree black belt in Kung Fu San Soo, and lived and breathed all things "fighting." Now my instructor did not teach or promote any of the ancient Chinese philosophies originating from their religion of Taoism. In fact, he only taught Kung Fu as a brutal street-fighting system. But I wanted more.

I wanted to be the best at Kung Fu, and so I sought to obtain additional power through the esoteric use of "Chi" energy and breathing meditation techniques. I mixed martial arts philosophies with my ancient American Indian New Age beliefs. Again, there are many New Age teachers using martial techniques like Tai Chi and other "internal" arts to promote their occult philosophies.

I sought more power. Studying Tai Chi and other internal arts, I found that controlling my breath, energy, and semen gave me more peace, balance, and a devastating punch. The big thing I did every day - I meditated. I would "stand like a tree" or "stand like a mountain" for an hour circulating the energy up from the earth into my energy meridians. Also, practicing moving meditation like Tai Chi and Kung Fu forms, I would empty my mind to receive the power of the Tao. To me, tapping into the Chinese concept of Chi was the same as tapping into the Native American concept of the Great Spirit. I could easily mix both New Age philosophies because they are all essentially the same.

Freemasonry

The third occurrence, which desensitized me to accept the occult and witchcraft, was my involvement with Free Masonry. Again, I was in my late thirties when I was exposed to Free Masonry through several police officers that were my friends and peers. I began to research Masonry and wanted to know its secrets, believing of course, it would give me power.

Masons cannot be recruited, a man must show interest and ask to join no less than three times in order to be invited to apply for membership. This I did, and I applied for membership and was accepted. There were three of us who were going to receive our "first degree" in Free Masonry, but not before asking several Christians their thoughts on Free Masonry. In fact, one of these men was a pastor of a church that had brothers who were Masons. Every Christian told me they saw no issue with me joining this "fraternity."

The night we were to start our Masonic journey was dark and rainy. There was a power outage and there were no lights on in the Masonic Lodge. The men decided to go through with the ritual anyway, by candlelight. I took my turn being inducted into Masonry, being led blindfolded around the Lodge declaring that what I wanted most was to "see the light." Of course, this refers to the Masonic "light" – the secrets of Masonic philosophy. At one point in the ritual, I was laying on the floor blindfolded from the beginning, and so had not seen anything or anyone around me. It was eerie.

The Lodge was pitch-black, except for a few candles flickering. It was cold, dark, and stormy outside, just like a horror movie. When they removed the blindfold from my eyes, the first man I saw was standing over me, wearing a tuxedo with a top hat. He appeared to be about eighty years old. He was mumbling some sort of Masonic mumbo jumbo with the light of the candles barely reflecting off his near dead white face. The first thing I thought was, "Am I in Hell?" I honestly believed that I could have been in Hell. It was a very eerie and creepy ritual, and I felt odd and disturbed.

I had a few issues with Masonry even as a "New Ager." For one, I did not like calling the leader of the Lodge "Worshipful Master" because I was not about to worship any man. I knew better. The other thing that bothered me was that Masons refer to their practices as "the Craft." This was too close to witchcraft for me. But, the men were very nice and sincere, so I continued to go through the other degrees.

I finally was "raised to the third degree" in Masonry, and was as much a Mason as anybody. I continued to attend and participate in rituals. One time, a Christian was receiving his first degree. After the ritual, he kept telling me that he "felt weird," and that something seemed wrong. I relieved his fears by telling him that the ritual is designed for shock value, but inside I always wondered if we had invited demons upon us.

As a police officer, the Masonic Lodge asked me to investigate new applicants. Every one was investigated in order to determine their character and suitability in the organization. It was illegal to use any law enforcement computer databases for such investigations, but it was not illegal for me to use my skills and knowledge to fully expose any candidate's potential to join our Lodge.

The police department had many high-ranking officials who were Masons. Some had been Masters of their Lodges. Joining these ranks certainly did not hurt me when it came time for promotions. There was a secret room in the Lodge, which contained numerous pictures of men on the walls. When I was shown this room, I saw portraits of many past police chiefs, district attorneys, judges, and other influential men in the county judicial system.

I took many blood oaths, and promised to die in the most bloodiest cruel manner if I ever revealed any of the secrets of Free Masonry. I cursed myself to have my throat cut, my entrails removed, and to be sheared in pieces. The birds would peck my eyes out and the wild animals would eat my flesh. I promised to be thrown into the sea if I revealed even the slightest secret of Masonry.

Blood oaths have to be renounced and broken to break the demonic tie into one's life. Years later, I would officially demit from the organization and repent for my sins. This was one fraternity I had to sever all ties with.

However, Masonry was not the only time a curse was spoken over me. In my early thirties, I was working the graveyard shift as a patrol officer. In a neighborhood well known for its drug and gang activity, my partner and I one night decided to arrest a man who was legendary regarding his evil and criminal behavior. Pound for pound, this man was one of the meanest individuals in the city. I will refer to him as "Rick." Every brother and sister had already died a violent death, and many people in the community blamed the family's involvement with Santeria.

The Curse

Santeria is an occult religion, like voodoo and other forms of paganism originally brought to America by some African slaves. Santeria mixes the worship of gods (idols) with Catholicism, which the name implies

23

"saint worship." One of the members of Rick's family was a Santeria priest.

On this particular cool February night, my partner and I investigated Rick for a trespassing violation. This contact with Rick turned into a fight when he resisted our attempts to take him into custody. Now police officers are legally allowed to use that amount of force necessary to overcome a person's resistance to arrest, and so that is what we did. However, we could not control Rick, or easily take him into custody. Why? Rick was under the influence of a drug known as PCP, which gave him superhuman strength and bravado. He felt no pain, and so getting compliance using pain techniques simply did not work.

A tiresome fight ensued. Unbeknownst to us, one of Rick's associates was about to strike my partner over the head with a metal pipe, but another man standing nearby stopped him from "killing a cop." The fight ended with Rick tragically dying in the end. As I stood up from the ground, fatigued and dizzy, I looked down on Rick's motionless body. I knew he was dead. He had died by our hands, and the feeling inside me was surreal. I still remember the shock I felt when a few weeks later the county coroner's report stated that Rick's cause of death was a "homicide," death by the hands of another.

As back-up officers and supervisors arrived, so did the neighborhood. I was surrounded by an angry mob taking flash photography while cursing me. A lady walked up to me after briefly staring me in the eyes, looked down at my torn and mangled uniform nametag. She then pronounced this curse upon me. In a calm determined voice she said, "Villanueva, I damn you to Hell! I curse your life." She then did the same to my partner. The lady, I would later find out, was Rick's mother.

Because of the possible exposure to PCP during the struggle, we went to the local hospital for treatment. Unfortunately, Rick's corpse went there also. When we arrived, there was a large crowd from the neighborhood in the parking lot. A young man chanting approached my partner and me. He was exercising what appeared to be animal bones in his hands. He was clearly doing incantations and spells. This young man was the Santeria priest.

About a week later, my partner's two-year old son suddenly came down with a high fever and quit walking. He never walked again. Through the years, doctors have not been able to accurately diagnose the illness. The boy's muscles just started to deteriorate. Prior to his son's fever, my partner had a vivid and frightening dream where he saw himself back at the hospital parking lot with the Santeria priest chanting a spell over him with "chicken bones" in his hands. My partner has always believed that the incident with Rick that night was related to his son's inability to ever walk again.

Years later, surgery after surgery, metal rods replacing metal rods, my partner's son is confined to a wheelchair. He had been a healthy, active, walking and running two-year old boy. It could be coincidence that he came down with a mysterious disease days after his father being cursed. It could be coincidence that he stopped walking the day his father had the vision of the Santeria priest casting a spell on him. It could be a coincidence that something very evil coming from my bedroom closet attacked me the very same night my partner saw his vision. But, I suspect it was not mere coincidence.

The same night my partner dreamed of the Santeria priest, Linda and I were home, smelling the smoke of a "wood fire." The smell was very strong and was only centered near our bed. It was so real, that I literally went around the house feeling the walls for the heat of a fire. I went outside and all around the house, but the smell of a wood fire was only around our bed. Both Linda and I smelled it. We went to sleep, and sometime in the night, Linda got up to use the restroom. As she passed her open closet door, something gave her the creeps. She felt as if something was inside the closet.

Not knowing Linda was already up, I made my way to the restroom also. As I passed the open closet, I felt something attack me from behind. I started screaming at the top of my lungs as I stumbled into the restroom with Linda. She looked at me and started screaming also because my face had changed. She said that my eyes were like "cat eyes" with a green vertical pupil with the white of the eyes bloodshot. I was foaming at the mouth. I remember being so terrified. The fear I felt was not like any other fear I have ever felt. We both do not remember the rest of that night.

For the next three days, I was extremely disturbed mentally. The next morning, I woke up very depressed and was crying. Linda wanted to stay home from work and be with me. I insisted that she go but later I would regret that decision. I felt like I was insane. Everything made me afraid and was eerie. I wanted to kill myself. Now remember, that the day before I was normal, but now I was suicidal for no reason at all. I was afraid of that closet for a long time.

My parents were out of town and I promised to go water their plants. As I went inside their home, I could not look at any pictures of family because I felt their eyes were following me around the room. Everything made me afraid, and I had to get back to my own home. It was the strangest thing I had ever experienced at that time. But, I suspected it had something to do with that curse placed on me. This deep depression and suicidal thoughts stayed with me for about three days before subsiding. I do not know why it left, but it did. I suspect it left by the grace of God. My partner was not so lucky.

Rebellion

The reader can understand that my involvement with the New Age in Native American and Chinese philosophies coupled with my participation with blatant satanic rituals in the Masonic Lodge made me a prime target for demonic deception. I cannot be sure the curse placed on me by Rick's family did not follow me into the years. Keep in mind; I was never an atheist or a pagan. I believed that I was a Christian, saved at age fifteen, and going to Heaven. At this time, I had already earned a Bachelor of Arts degree in Biblical Studies with a minor in Systematic Theology. But, I did not know God. I did not know what the Word of God taught. I was a cultural Christian raised in church, but now living in rebellion, which is as the seed of witchcraft.

There were three other areas in my life that catapulted me into Satan's arms.

1. I quit regularly reading and studying Scripture for many years. Instead, I read and studied occult material. When I did read the Bible, I approached it intellectually and refused to actually live the principles contained in them. Along the lines of refusing Biblical truth, I also refused to have anything to do with "Christians" in or out of a church setting. Because I hated church and its people so much, I had no accountability, no brotherhood, no family, and no leadership to teach me. I was on my own.

If anyone would suggest that I go to church, I would blast back with the fact that going to church is not a condition of salvation. One of the greatest lies I believed was that I could serve and worship God on my own terms and in my own way without the religious culture of a church hampering me.

2. Jesus was not the Lord of my life rather I was lord of my life. I was concerned only with earthly success

driven by my pride and arrogance. I was ego centric and self-centered. I really believed I was stronger, smarter, and superior to others. I was a trained fighter and shooter, and feared no man physically or intellectually. Everything I did with passion was to obtain power. I wanted power, money, success, and respect.

In my thirties, Linda and I owned many rental properties, cars, and material things. We had five mortgages, two Harley Davidson motorcycles, several automobiles, a beautiful home, custom landscaping and furniture, and every modern technological device imaginable. And I was promoting at work and desiring even more power and money.

3. I rejected any form of suffering or discipline from God, and withdrew from any attempt to mold or make me into the image of Jesus. I had no understanding about becoming like Christ through the sanctification process, nor did I want any understanding. I had received Christ at age fifteen, and that was enough. Sin to me was relative. When God would reach out to me, I would run. I was complacent to be who I was, earthly minded, and carnal.

Complimenting my eroding Christianity, I finally had an extra-marital affair. Because I had justified all of my sinful conduct in the past, having an affair was not a big leap for me. Additionally, because I was running away from God, I was unprotected from the severity of my enemy, Satan. He would have received great pleasure first destroying my life and then consuming my soul.

I committed adultery with a woman practicing dark arts of the occult. Like me, she had esoteric beliefs about reincarnation, the dead, spirit guides, and other occult beliefs. She practiced Wicca, and considered herself highly "spiritual" and connected to the "ancients" through reincarnation and conversations with the dead. Although she used metaphysical techniques to draw me to her, I was just as much to blame in first creating her within my own lustful mind. Even if I did so inadvertently, I had fabricated this person in my thoughts and the demons were more than happy to bring the two of us together.

I was away from home on a police related business trip, disillusioned, angry, and wanting to stay drunk the night I met this other woman. I was in the hotel lounge with some friends drinking and partying when she walked in and ordered something at the bar. We started talking with her and I shook her hand as she sat down with us. In a few days, she would tell me that the moment she shook my hand, she felt as if I was falling and I needed rescuing. This was the beginning of my obsessive belief that she was "saving" me from something.

She would also convince me that her dead father communicated with her the same night before our meeting. He told her that he had a "gift" for her in the bar and that she needed to leave her room and go to the hotel lounge to claim it. I was her gift from her dead father. Because I was into the spiritual aspect of the occult and fascinated with death, I was impressed by her story rather than fearful or alarmed.

30

A "Jinni" or "jinn" is an evil or familiar spirit that can influence and control a person. My adulterous affair was with a woman who openly admitted that she considered herself part demon and part human. She stated she was one quarter "Jinni" or "Genie." She boasted in having the same attributes and characteristics of this particular demon. And this is what I got involved with. I considered myself a Christian with a good handle on Scripture, yet one can see that I was far removed from God and any true Biblical Christianity.

Spell Casting

Now I am not saying, "The devil made me do it," because I am to blame for placing myself in such a dangerous situation. But, here is what happened to me. After having just one sexual encounter with her, I totally and whole-heartedly fell in love with her in just 13 mini-dates! She literally "taught" me how to conduct an illicit affair. Using code names (one of her names was from a Tarot card and another from a demonic entity), Emails, cellular telephone text messages, music CDs, and secrecy, she set up an elaborate system of constant communication with me.

Immediately, this "virtual" online affair took off. Although it would be another three weeks before I physically saw her again, I became totally mesmerized and spellbound with this woman. From this point on, we will refer to her name as Riana. I was bewitched, and longed for her even though I honestly could not remember what she looked like!

She related that her spirit animal was a crow, and although it seems strange now, I would have crows following me everywhere I went. And of course whenever I saw a crow, I would think of her and long for her.

She sent me music CDs, which she compiled. The songs on these disks were not songs that I would normally like, but I was drawn to the music. This was bewitching music with whispers and vampire-like lyrics that I would hear in my sleep. But, other times, the music was from popular rock bands. I constantly listened to the various CDs she would mail to me. The more I listened to them, the deeper in "love" I fell.

The music would make me sad and yearn for her. It was addicting. These songs took a hold of me emotionally. Songs about her came to me in my dreams. She came to me in my dreams. Interestingly, one of the song lyrics talked about a woman "saving" a man. In the song, the man asks the woman if he is worth saving. Well, this theme of her being my savior was embedded deep into my psyche, and would constantly surface. The music was so powerful that even after I had broken it off with her, I could not be in any place that was playing one of these songs without becoming extremely hypnotized. This followed me for months afterward. It probably took me a year or so before I could hear these songs without becoming emotional about them.

Every waking moment I thought of her. I felt like I had known her for years. Within a matter of a few short weeks, I considered her my best friend. I needed constant daily contact from her, and when at times she did not communicate to me, I went crazy inside and felt frantic. Keep in mind I only met her once, and all of this is happening between our first encounter and three weeks later to the second encounter. This is absolutely amazing, and I had no idea how bizarre my behavior had become. At the time, I was completely unaware of what was happening to me.

On one occasion, her cellular telephone was broken, and she did not contact me for several days. When she finally reconnected to me, I was in a panic - a sheer panic. She apologized and said, "I should have known better." At the time, I did not know what she meant by this statement, but now I know that it was part of the spell casting and binding ritual. Her withdrawal from me was designed to test the strength of her love spell on me, and to ascertain if it was working properly.

During the three weeks between our first and second meetings, I missed her so much that I compared my "longing" for her to feelings I had when my own father died. Literally, I had not felt such grief and sadness since my father's death, and now I was comparing that feeling to missing this unknown woman. How could I have ignored these red flags of danger? Truly, I was deluded.

When I saw her again for a few days while on a business trip, she took total control of everything. She would drive us everywhere, select the restaurants, open doors for me (including the car door), and make all arrangements for everything. She continually "doted" over me like a pet. She treated me as a man would treat a woman he was courting.

Strangely, she handed me a package that contained satellite photographs of my house and property, the amount of money I paid, owed, and what it was worth. She said she needed to know the person she was dealing with. All these things go against my nature. Normally, I would have run the opposite direction, but I was in a "stupor" around her and just relaxed into everything. She also encouraged my drunkenness, and I was always drinking heavy around her.

After seeing her only the second time, I was convinced that we were past lovers from a past life. We talked about reincarnation, and I was convinced that she was my true love over again in multiple past lives. She talked about spiritualism, Buddhism, reincarnation, and metaphysics. She convinced me that the "universe" and its energy brought us back together as it always has in our other lives. But, this time we were to stay together forever. She read the Tarot cards and conducted positive readings over our relationship. I examined and learned about Tarot cards on the Internet because of her suggestions. I also personally consulted the Chinese oracle the I-Ching for answers and confirmation.

The third time I saw her, she was going to divorce her husband and had "plans" for us. She had travel plans, living arrangements, and all the details worked out. She had a close girl friend and traveling companion that was an admitted witch and lesbian. This friend dressed and lived as a vampire, and she considered herself a real vampire. She had a gothic decorated house and hung around other occult practitioners in various "vampire nightclubs." And this was the house where we were going to stay when we both left our spouses. I had decided that I wanted to be with her, and was about to walk away from my 16-year marriage with Linda.

Keep in mind that all of this occurred within a short three-months span of meeting her. I had known of this Riana for a total of 180 days. Later, I figured out the actual time I had spent with her was 13 days, and all of those days were partial days. I estimate I had actually spent about 40-hours with this Riana. I did not realize this until after I was rescued. At the time, it seemed that I had known this woman for a very long time, a very powerful spell indeed.

My life was a shambles. I had entered into a "danger house" and began a torturous cycle of pain. My stressful job and my uneventful marriage made me feel alone. I was not connected to any church congregation and had no spiritual support. I felt distant from my wife with our lives taking on separate avenues. She had her friends, and I had none. I had lost all means to have fun or romance in our relationship, and replaced sex with my wife with Internet pornography, and this removed me even farther away from her. We could not communicate with each other. Although pleasant and cordial, we did not want to be around each other.

Because of my constant anger and irritation, Linda removed herself from me, causing me to feel more isolated, which caused her to retreat farther, and so the vicious cycle continued. This isolation or aloneness was fueled by my extreme emotions of hate and anger. I hated everyone. I simply hated people. Highly critical of every human I came in contact with, I isolated myself from humanity in general.

Of course, I wanted nothing to do with people in a church, because I had lost all faith and hope in "Christians" and organized religion. Besides, I did not think I needed organized religion because I was spiritual within myself. The aloneness and extreme emotions caused me to turn to alcohol as a stress reliever. I liked the way I was numbed to some degree when I was drunk. Of course, eventually the drug only intensified my already extreme loneliness and anger, and loosened my inhibitions to carry out my fantasies.

Maybe it was guilt, I am not sure, but I had to be drunk in order to be with this Riana. She also encouraged my drunken stupor and made sure I was always in a relaxed state. It seemed to me that I was always more than just intoxicated by alcohol. Rather, I was in a fog-like condition. I can remember hearing "whispering" words in my ear while I was barely conscious. These same whisperings would continue to haunt me for months even after I was rescued from this relationship. The voices always came while I was in a dream-like, fog-induced state of consciousness.

The other part of this danger house is non-confession, secrecy, or hidden things. I did not communicate with my wife nor did I confess my sins to her or to God. I had dozens of secrets like my pornography collection, my alcohol abuse, and this illicit affair. Men, if you have a "secret stash" of money, pornography, pictures of old girlfriends, or anything else that you are keeping a secret from your wife, then you are in danger. There are to be no secrets in your marriage. Period. Ladies, that goes for you also. Get rid of all secret things now. Your spouse should not "find" any secret things about you if you were to suddenly die tomorrow.

All of these things like habitual secrecy, extreme emotions, altering the mind through drugs or alcohol, and loneliness are the building blocks of a danger house. If you or your spouse may be displaying any of these building blocks, then your marriage is in grave danger and needs intervention immediately.

Linda knows all too well how the building blocks of sin can infect a marriage, and open the door to major demonic influences. Later, as I began to heal, I did not remember many things I had said and done. I cannot remember being this bad and hateful, as I was very mentally deluded. As I heard her side of the story regarding my behavior, I was shocked. This all seemed so out of character for me. My behavior was controlled, or at least heavily influenced by a demonic presence.

About this time, we had a housekeeper suddenly quit. She had worked for us for several years. Although, I never spoke to her since the day I hired her, I always felt she was frightened of me. Today, I believe this is the reason why she left. Now I realize that at times I was displaying a very evil and hateful presence. I remember going to the store, and having people reacting to me as if they were frightened. I thought it was because I exuded self-confidence and command presence. I would have never believed it was a spirit of anger surrounding and oppressing me. But I was always angry. I simply hated humans.

In fact, after I returned to Christ, a Christian friend at work that I had known for years told me that I used to look at him so hatefully that it made him nervous. He would ask other people who knew me what was wrong with me, and they just made excuses for me. He told me of specific times that I just gave him the most hateful looks of distain. To my amazement, I had no recollection of ever feeling any animosity toward this man, or looking hateful at him. He was seeing the demonic influence emanate from me, and I was very unaware of the affect I was having on others, including my wife. The following is Linda's story about my demonic behavior during this very strange period, and she will narrate from this point on.

Demonic Behavior

At this point in time, Paul and I (Linda) were married sixteen years, but we had been friends for about twenty-six years. During the last two years, our marriage began to quickly deteriorate. Our lack of communication was basically the straw that broke the camel's back. We had lost all forms of intimacy, essential for a healthy marriage: physical, spiritual and emotional. Looking back, the pivotal point that started to rock our marital foundation occurred when Paul was promoted to the rank of police lieutenant. His new job assignment made him very unhappy. He felt trapped. Every day he would come home angry and frustrated. Months later, his disposition continued during his days off.

As part of management, he was issued a "Smart Phone" device, which connected him to his work continuously. He became obsessed and was constantly on it. He was either checking his emails or sending them, or he was answering calls or making them. He checked his machine every twenty to thirty minutes. It began to cut into our family time. We were hopeful that his next assignment would be better, but it was not. He went from one frying pan into another, which made his anger and frustration worse. By this time, he started drinking at home. He became reclusive even with me. We no longer had conversations, just one-sided dialog and it was coming from his end. Whenever I would make a suggestion or interject something, he would snap.

I could not say anything without making him angry with me, which caused me to walk on eggshells. I was very careful with what I said or when I said something. Paul was unpleasant to be around all the time now. I was lonely for him, but he did not have time for me. Since my husband's bad mood and rejections made it clear to me that he did not want me around, I would go out with my friends. I had one particular friend whom I had recently met that I got along with very well. I will call her Diana. We became inseparable. She had a family, but her husband was also always working. She filled the void that was missing between Paul and me. The irony of it all was that whatever we did together made me think of Paul and how I wished we could share the moment. I felt lonesome for my husband.

One time Paul called me from the road, and said he was on his way home and wanted to know what I was doing. I told him I was having lunch with Diana, and he surprised me when he said he wanted to join us. Something did not feel right to me. That was not like him. Plus, I detected sarcasm and arrogance in his voice. When he arrived at the restaurant, he was arrogant and rude. I knew something was up, but I could not put my finger on it. His behavior towards me was aggressive and I was embarrassed by it. My stomach began to tighten up and I felt very uncomfortable having him there. Our calm atmosphere instantly changed into tension.

After lunch, I said good-bye to my friend and then Paul walked me to my car. Immediately, I felt his demeanor change. When I told him I would meet him at home, he said he had to wash his car and go to the cleaners. That raised a red flag for me. Paul is a person of habit. Normally, he would have gone straight home from his trip and I would take his clothes to the cleaners. Paul's car would have had to be excessively dirty for him to go to the car wash, which it was not. Paul normally has he car washed while he is at work. Something was not right. When I got home, Diana called me. She said she did not like Paul's behavior and she was concerned for my safety. She said she saw a side to him that scared her, and she was frightened of him for me. His arrogance and rudeness was not anything new to me, so I was not frightened.

When he returned home, he was cool and distant. He did not have much to say to me. He was more interested in answering his Emails. I let him alone. He did his usual clean up after a trip, but he was not very communicative with me. That was unusual for him. As the days went by, he started acting like himself again. We also had to get ready for the family reunion party we were hosting that weekend. But, after the family reunion, Paul became very distant towards me. It only drove me farther away from him. I was either going to school or going out with Diana. Whenever I touched Paul, his body became rigid. He had no life in his eyes. There were times he would look at me with such distain. I felt he did not love me anymore. I had this feeling that Paul hated me. He was behaving hateful towards me. If looks could kill, I would have been dead. He did not like me touching him and he would snarl at me as I walked passed him.

I started to suspect he might be having an affair, but that thought seemed so ludicrous. I had always trusted Paul. He never gave me reason not to. Besides, his personality would not consider such an option no matter how unhappy he was with our marriage. Paul was a person of habit and I could not imagine him divided by two women. That lifestyle would be too stressful for Paul. He was a creature of habit. I always said one could set a watch to him. Additionally, I was confident enough to believe that not too many women would put up with his peculiar character traits as I did.

The more I thought about Paul having an affair, the more I was convinced he was not having one. However, I could not shake the feeling something was definitely wrong. One evening, he sat on the couch to watch television. I sat beside him and reached for his hand. He removed his hand away from mine while having a blank stare at the television. I asked him if he was planning to leave me. He gave me a scrawl and said no in disgust and then got up and left the room. He did not ask me why I would ask such a question, nor did he try to convince me he was not leaving.

I knew something was wrong, and it scared me. He retreated to his home recording studio and he was recording something. When I entered the room, I startled him. He then rattled off how he felt inspired to play after playing guitar with his uncles at the family reunion. The odd thing was Paul worked with his headphones on, and he did not share with me what he was working on. Normally, Paul played his music loud, and he would play his music for me. Now, he did not even want to share this anymore.

The Sign and Omens

That following weekend there was a snake in our bedroom. This was the beginning of many actual snakes seen in our house. Paul was walking by our bedroom when he saw movement in the corner of his eye. As he quickly looked, he saw the tail of a large black snake slither under our bed. He immediately called for me and had me stand guard at our bedroom door while he tried to find the snake. Together we managed to empty the entire room except for two small nightstands and the bed itself. Yet, still no snake was found. It was as if it just disappeared.

We cleared the entire area under the bed and removed the mattress and box spring from the room, but no snake was present. There was only one small nightstand left, which was located at Paul's side of the bed. It was his nightstand. As he carefully lifted up the nightstand, the floor beneath it was void of any snake. It had vanished, so we thought. Then Paul opened all of the nightstand drawers, and still no snake. What happened? How could this animal be so deceptive, and so concealing?

As Paul examined the furniture thoroughly, he suddenly saw the snake wrapped up around one of the wooden beams that separated the nightstand drawers. He picked up the nightstand, and placed it outside while opening the drawers. Then a large black snake slithered out, and found its way into some brush. We had never had a snake in the house before this incident, and have never had one in our bedroom since this event. This was a sign. It was a warning. The symbolism of a large black snake slithering under my marriage bed was obvious. Yet, at the time, I was still uncertain that Paul was going deeper and deeper into the dark world of Satan. I later found out that Paul had slipped away that very afternoon to meet his mistress.

Another significant omen was the barn owls we had living above our bedroom ceiling, nesting in a deep crevice where the outside patio cover and house eaves met. About one-year before Paul's slide into darkness, we heard strange noises in our bedroom. One such noise sounded just like "breathing" or "hissing" and it seemed to emanate from the corner of Paul's side of the bed! It was frightening until we discovered that some barn owls had decided to nest above our bed. Late at night (when owls are active), we were awakened by loud bangs and thumps at our window. When we looked outside, we would see young owls clinging onto our window screen and flapping their wings. This was a common occurrence until Paul returned to God, and then suddenly the owls stopped nesting above our bedroom and have not returned since. At the time, several people had warned us that this was not a "good omen," but we thought it was just a natural animal occurrence.

My sister-in-law had a dream. She dreamed that her brother, Paul, was having an extra marital affair. She dreamed it twice! The dream was so real and vivid to her that she actually confronted Paul about it. Paul became irritated at her accusation, vehemently denying such a thing. Yet, just two months later, he was in fact having an affair.

At the time of the dream, the thought of Paul having an affair was so absurd that we laughed about it. However, now I was having second thoughts and yet, I could not believe he would cheat on me for several reasons. First,

I know Paul, and he was not easy to live with. Years of police work, undercover narcotics assignments, killing a man, and now management stress had made him a little nutty. Second, needy people irritated him, especially needy women. Third, he is a man of routine and he gets easily frustrated when his routine is disrupted. Fourth, Paul and I had a history of over 20 years together, and recently went through the grief of some very personal losses to death - his dad and both my parents.

Yet, his demonic behavior fulfilled that omen of a dream his sister had. That dream and its urgency was also a sign to both of us. A sign largely ignored at the time. If a large black snake slithering under my marriage bed was a clear symbolic representation of the dark evil that was about to overtake us, then the plain, simple, and very realistic dream of my husband engaging in an illicit affair was a quaking shout to wake up out of our deep spiritual sleep.

Paul was conducting his affair in a city about two-hours away from where we lived. He traveled a lot on business, and this was the perfect guise in hiding his new relationship. Just a day before Paul left for an out-of-town trip, I had a dream about a sick puppy I nursed to health. Then I had another dream about a bird. In the first dream, I was holding a little frail chocolate brown Chihuahua puppy. This little dog was very ill, and I was nursing it back to health. Later on, this dream would come true. When Paul returned to me, he was extremely sick both spiritually and emotionally. It took a long time and much patience to bring him back into a

45

state of wellness. Then the second dream was of a special bird that flew into our house, and I managed to help the bird escape from its torment.

Now, Paul often times can interpret dreams, and many people have consulted him in the past about the meaning of significant dream events. Oddly enough, he cannot interpret his own dreams. I told my dreams to him and watched his reaction. I was stunned when he said he did not know what the dreams meant. I knew he had lied to me, but why? What did these dreams or signs mean to him, and why would he not share his thoughts with me? I knew the dreams were significant, but I had no idea the magnitude until a few days later. Again, these dreams were signs to both of us. The obvious symbolism of a sick puppy and a lost bird related to my husband's deadly sins.

Paul had left on his final "business trip," and I felt very uneasy. My stomach was in knots and something was not right. I went to my prayer closet and talked to God. I told Him again about my suspicions and how sorry I was, but that I could not shake this feeling. I asked God to help me find anything that would confirm or deny my feelings that Paul was having an affair. I said, "God, if my suspicions are real, please show me a sign. But if my feelings are unfounded, then please remove these nagging suspicions and forgive me." After I prayed, I walked around the house and I suddenly remembered the night I caught him off guard in the recording studio.

I went into the studio and I noticed a blank yellow notepad on the table. As I leafed through it, a green steno paper fell out from between the pages. I picked it up and turned it over and there were words written on it. I recognized Paul's writing. It was a poem. It was the lyrics to the song he was writing. Whenever Paul liked someone, he expressed his feelings in song. All at once, I realized he was having an affair and this sexually explicit song was written for her. The song was about one of their rendezvous encounters at the hotel he was staying. Immediately, my world came crashing down, my knees went weak and I dropped to the floor, calling out to God, "Oh my God, I can't believe this. What should I do?" It was one of the most painful feelings of betrayal that I had ever felt. I sobbed from deep within my soul. My heart was broken. A flood of different emotions surfaced. I felt pain, betrayal, fear, anger, and guilt.

Then, I started to doubt my reasoning and felt that may be I misread it. Through my tears, I read the lyrics several times over. Each time it became more difficult for me to understand. My body was shaking, my stomach was tight and I felt nausea. I had to get another opinion, so I called my sister. After I read the note to her, she immediately advised me to throw out all his stuff and change the locks. I also called my close friend who gave me similar advice. I wanted to contact his family, but I could not hurt them with this news.

While I was on the phone with my sister, I could tell another caller was trying to get through. I surmised it was Paul, but he could call back later. What was odd was that Paul immediately called my cellular telephone

47

number. He does not normally do that. I put my sister on hold to take the call. He was in good spirits. He told me that he arrived safely and gave me his room number, but he asked me not to call his room because he would be out. I knew he was going to be with "her." It broke my heart simultaneously making me sick.

I prayed and asked God to help me. I asked for forgiveness because I felt may be I was partly to blame for Paul's infidelity. I was not angry with Paul anymore. It takes two people to make a marriage, and if he did this, there had to be a reason. I had lots of time to think. I was remembering the warning signs: My sister-in-law's dream about Paul's infidelity, his comments about specific members of his family being womanizers and how it must be an inevitable trait, buying new clothes, watching his weight and the change of attitude. Of course, I could not forget the owls waking us up at night, the snake under our marriage bed, and my dreams as well.

The Rescue

I wanted to go where Paul was, but the Lord had me wait for a while. I contacted my friend who had experience with an unfaithful husband. She and her therapist strongly advised me to get proof of Paul's infidelity. According to them, husbands have a way of denying their affairs. They did not approve of me going on my own to get proof, but suggested I retain an investigator to follow Paul and take pictures.

I contacted a friend of mine who did private investigations. Since my friend met Paul once, he was concerned that Paul would recognize him, so he suggested a colleague of his to do the investigation. My friend said this would take a little time to set up.

The Lord was my strength and my comfort. Because I was still attending college, He gave me the strength to go to my classes and complete the assignments. I trusted the Lord, but it was a long week. My friend, Diana, told me that I did not look good. I looked tired and pale. She cautioned me not to look that way when Paul got home for he would suspect me. I listened to the advice people were giving me, but I always went to the Lord and inquired of Him. I knew He was working in my heart and I found that I was standing on the Scripture, Galatians 2:20, that I had memorized a year before. It reads that "I no longer live, but Christ lives in me." I prayed that God would pour His Holy Spirit in my heart for Paul and for this woman.

I was not angry with Paul, but had compassion and forgiveness. Paul was not only my husband, but he was my friend and my brother in Christ. I would stick by him, but if he wanted to leave me then I knew God would take care of me. I did not want to lose Paul or have our marriage become another divorce statistic. Whenever I would have thoughts of our demise, I would go to the Lord in prayer and He gave me strength and hope through His Word and Holy Spirit. It was God and His Word that provided the ultimate signs for me -

signs that pointed toward hope, forgiveness, and salvation.

Paul was gone for an entire week, and I knew he was coming home the following day, so I reasoned that I could wait and talk with him then. But, I felt an urgency that I needed to confront him sooner. I was unsure what I needed to do. Again, I prayed and asked God for guidance. After attending my morning class, I asked the Lord what I needed to do. I kept my lunch date with my friend, Cheryl.

I was surprised how peaceful I was during lunch. Somehow we started talking about my suspicions and how I planned to go to Paul's location and see for myself, if he was with another woman or not. My friend assured me that Paul was too ethical to have an affair. She suggested that I wait until the next day, and talk to him about my insecurities. She was confident that all would be well. It made sense to me and I resolved at that moment that I would follow her advice. However, on my way home, I had that urgent feeling that I should not wait, but go and see Paul today. Confusion filled my heart, "Lord, what do you want me to do?"

When I got home, I left a message with my investigator friend, and I prayed until I had heard from the Lord. The investigator returned my call. He said that his colleague could start the investigation the following week. I told him that Paul was coming home tomorrow and I needed to know tonight. Paul was scheduled for another "business trip" next month, but I could not wait that long. I would go crazy. I told him that I planned to confront Paul today.

When he realized my determination, he gave me some good advice. He asked me what I planned to do after I caught him. I did not have an answer. I never thought past that moment. He prepared me for the worst. He said if Paul was with another woman and I saw that, it would hurt and he was concerned how I would react. He feared for my safety. He cautioned me to take a friend along, but if I could not get a friend to come with me that I should get a hotel room before confronting Paul. He did not think I should be driving afterwards. He also suggested that if Paul was not with another woman that I stay with him that night and return home with him in the morning. Just because she is not with him at that moment, does not mean she would not be coming later on.

As he was talking to me, I suddenly became overwhelmingly conscious of my body. The realization that Paul could be having an affair hit me at that moment. I felt my stomach tighten, my mouth was dry, and my entire body was shaking uncontrollably. The thought that I could lose Paul and our marriage made me feel sick to my stomach. In an instant, I felt numb and my world seemed so surreal. "My God, I'm afraid. This cannot be happening. What do you want me to do?"

I felt anxious and I paced around my house, praying and listening for God's voice. What seemed like hours were only a few minutes, then I felt a peace come over me, and the Lord spoke to my heart. He said, "Go, and I will reveal to you what you need to know." I called my sister to pray for me, and I called another friend nearby for precautionary purposes. She offered to come with me, but I felt that I needed to do this on my own. I quickly prepared an overnight bag, received driving directions from the computer, and headed out the door.

The moment I got in my car I felt peace, joy, and strength. I had the assurance in my heart that everything was going to be all right. The Lord told me to take my time, get in the slow lane, and to set my cruise control. I left in the early evening and it took me two hours to get to the hotel. I panicked when I saw the hotel. I was expecting a singular hotel building with floor levels. Instead, this hotel had bungalows. How was I going to find his room in the dark? As I prayed for God's help, I believe an angel was assigned to guide me because I felt my car was on autopilot and the steering wheel move on its own.

Before I knew it, I was at Paul's bungalow. I recognized his car and my stomach tightened a little. I had to remind myself to breathe. I parked on the opposite end of Paul's room and I backed in so I could keep watch. The light in Paul's room was on. I wondered if they were in there together. "What should I do, Lord?" He told me to wait.

I waited and watched the people go back and forth. It was busy. It was a beautiful and romantic place overlooking the water. I felt envious of this woman. I should be with my husband, not her. I started imagining what she must look like, but the Lord told me not to entertain those thoughts. After thirty minutes passed, the Lord told me to call him. I was surprised he was not in his room. He said he was having dinner with a male co-worker named Ralph. He said it sarcastically, and I knew she was "Ralph." I imagined her laughing at my expense. He asked me what I wanted. I told him that I missed him and wanted to see what he was doing. He said he was having delicious bass for dinner and some drinks. I told him I was glad he was enjoying himself, but when I said I loved him, he did not respond except for a grunt. Then he said good-bye and we hung up.

I later learned that he suspected that I knew about her and he felt that I was there waiting for him. I waited two hours for them. I saw her walking to his room and I began to blink my eyes because I did not want to miss anything. I was alert. She was not at all what I expected her to look like. She was not Paul's type at all, so I surmised that it had to be her personality.

Dread came over me as he quickly spotted me. I was disappointed that I would not be able to make my dramatic entrance into their love nest. He was walking over to me as she waited by his hotel room. As I opened my car door, he reeked of alcohol and I noticed the deadness in his eyes. There was no life in them. My heart broke and I wondered what happened to him.

He asked me what I was doing there. I told him that I wanted to surprise him. I asked him if she, pointing to her, was "Ralph," and he confirmed it was. When I looked at her, I discerned she lacked confidence. That knowledge gave me the advantage for the moment. I told him I wanted to meet her. I was still his wife and I had a right to talk with her. As I got out of the car and started walking towards her, she ran away.

I had to know if he loved her because that would determine whether I stay and fight, or go home and end our marriage. I asked him sternly, "Do you love her?" To my I surprise, he did not declare his love for her, but instead, only said he cared for her very much. Had he said he loved her, I would have gone home. He then suggested that we go for a walk and talk about the situation. He talked and I listened. I could sense something was not right with him. He reminded me of a zombie. He was emotionless. He was not behaving right. Several times, I would ask him to stop and look at me. His eyes glazed over, and he had a faraway look in his eyes. I could not get over the lifelessness in them.

He told me that she came into his life when he needed someone to save him, and she saved him. He said that she was his lifeline and that she told him that they were past lovers and were destined to meet. She knew Paul was married when she seduced him but she did not care. I noticed he wasn't wearing his wedding ring and it reminded me of the times when I asked him about it, he said it made him uncomfortable. It bothered his hand.

I also remembered the time he came to the restaurant where I was having lunch with my friend Diana, after one of his business trips. Diana said she had seen a vision of Paul putting on his wedding ring before entering the restaurant. After the rescue, I told him about this incident, and he told me that he did in fact do that. He said that before he came inside the restaurant, he opened his glove compartment, took out the ring, and put it on his finger. He told me Riana did not like it when he wore his wedding ring. In fact, she did not like it when Paul spoke of me. She even told him not to contact me when they were together.

Through all of this, I could not believe how calm I was. The Lord placed in my heart so much love and compassion for Paul. This moment was bathed in my prayers months before. Galatians 2:20 came to mind, "I no longer live, but Christ lives in me." Although Paul was in some sort of stupor beyond alcohol intoxication, he agreed to leave the hotel and come home with me. The other woman had disappeared for the moment.

Paul drove his car in front of me while I followed behind. I remember feeling very scared for Paul and sensing that he was in a very dark place. I just started praying to God. What I did not know was that Paul was having overwhelming and uncontrollable urges to drive off the road into the surrounding mountainside, thus killing himself. Later, he told me that as he was driving home, he kept envisioning himself letting go of the steering wheel, placing his hands above his head, and simply allowing the car to go careening off the highway into the deep crevices below. He said he could not understand why he did not do it, but suddenly he found himself at home.

Chapter 3: The Battle Begins

Divination

If the affair had not been bizarre enough, the aftermath following this marital mudslide was out of this world. Literally, this is when the demons with all of their evil started playing out their agenda.

Paul had later recounted how his mistress read the Tarot regarding their future. The first reading was positive, so she said, but Paul thought that she was not telling him something. The second reading took place right at the time he was going to end his marriage and go live with her. This reading was bad. The Tarot showed the worst calamity and fall for Paul if he were to go through with the illicit relationship. It concerned him, but not enough to stop his actions toward destruction. He justified the reading as pointing to the calamity of his family rejecting his new lover. He did not care.

Now at home, Paul had to make some drastic decisions whether to stay in his marriage or leave. Being into the occult, he consulted his ancient Chinese oracle, the I-Ching, or the Book of Changes. As he sat on the floor with three coins and his oracle book, he firmly held the coins in both hands while he intently asked the oracle this question, "Would it be beneficial or not for me to leave my wife and go with this other woman?" Whatever the reading would have revealed from the tossed coins, was what Paul would have accepted. He had a lot of faith in the I-Ching, and only consulted it on the most important matters in his life. This was serious business.

He threw his first three coins, and started building one of six hexagrams that would determine his future. After building the hexagrams, he consulted the Book of Changes for the proper interpretation and occult meanings of his throws. He would have done whatever the oracle led him to do. But, to his surprise the oracle gave off a very bad reading to his question. He would have faced certain destruction, if he left his marriage for his mistress. Just like the Tarot reading previously, the I-Ching warned him of extreme danger.

Additionally, before coming home, this Wiccan woman had a dream about Paul. She told him how bothered she was regarding this dream, and said it was very real and serious. She saw Satan dragging Paul into hell, behind a shut door. However, she then told him that she was able to grab him and save him from the "big guy's" clutches. Even then, Paul was not sure about the truth behind the second part of this dream.

Warnings were everywhere. Even the occult divinations were screaming at him. Yet, Paul was in a stupor. It was good that he was home, and at least had a fighting chance for his marriage, and ultimately his soul.

Spell Binding

The night of Paul's rescue was tense because we did not realize at that time the extent of demonic influence and control over him. At this point, we thought this was just an "affair" not realizing that it went so much deeper than just an ordinary marital affair. Once we got home, we sat and talked until the early morning hours. The other woman was confident that Paul would end his marriage and then return to her as soon as possible, she was not calling his telephone or attempting to contact him at all.

As we sat at the kitchen table, I listened as he talked about how much she meant to him. He began to cry. He was confused, sad, and felt very sorry for her. He repeated how he could not hurt her, as she was his "lifeline" and had "saved" him from falling. He told me that she was everything to him and it hurt him to be away from her. He showed visible signs of distress. His eyes were fearful and full of pain. His posture slumped over. My heart broke for him. Here was my best friend in so much pain, so the most loving thing I could do was release him with my blessing. I said, "Paul, if she means that much to you, then you should go to her. Life is too short. I do not want you to ever feel guilty about leaving me because God will take care of me, so do not worry about me, I will be all right. I release you with my blessing."

Immediately after I said that, he stopped crying, his expression changed from sorrowful to sober. It was as if another person suddenly took over Paul. It was as if he woke up from a dream. He then turned to me and said, "No, I want to stay here with you. Let's see if we can get some counseling." At that moment, the Lord revealed to me Paul was under a spell.

It seemed that the longer Paul was away from Riana, the more clarity he had, as if her magic was becoming weaker. We talked honestly and he told me everything. He would go in and out of crying spells and sorrow for her, but at least we were communicating. I told Paul that he had to break it off completely with Riana. I knew he had to sever all demonic ties with her in order to regain clarity of mind and spirit. He did. He sent her an Email and told her he was staying with his marriage. This did not come easy for him. He cried and hesitated, and said that pushing the send button was the hardest thing he has ever done. Then his telephone and Emails lit up. She was trying desperately to contact him. She was frantic. She was devastated that Paul had hurt her, ruined their plans, and she could not believe he was able to just walk away from her.

That night, in the twilight hours, Paul woke up and felt her strong presence in our house. He knew she was outside in her car at the driveway waiting to "save" him. He felt so strong about this that he actually got up and looked for her. He was peeking out of the window blinds like a little girl waiting for a date. He was nervous and antsy. I also felt her strong presence. I knew she was in our house, in our living room. I got up and confronted her spirit, and shouted, "Get out of our house!" Inside my head, I heard her laughing at me as she left.

When we went out to the garage, we saw a snake slither across the garage door threshold. This was the second manifestation of a snake since Paul's rescue. The one before this occurred while we drove home on the night of his rescue. I noticed a snake slink across our driveway. I remembered that Paul told me Riana hated snakes, and so at the time, I believed these snake manifestations came for our protection.

Her presence was so real it was freakish for sure. Was she projecting herself into our home? It certainly appeared that way. It was 2:00 AM when these strange things occurred, and that was just the beginning of our 2:00 AM nightmares. For several months, we were tormented with strange occurrences.

Then the next morning after all this high strangeness, Paul woke up and suddenly said, "It's magic." He said it was revealed to him in a dream that he was under magical influence. His eyes were clear and he seemed normal. Yet, he would go in and out of a trance-like state throughout the day. He would start talking about her and become "weepy" and sad. In order to break free from her influence, Paul had to delete all of her emails and telephone messages she had sent him, and every time he did this, he felt such guilt for hurting her. He was very tormented. It was difficult to witness.

Paul could not be left alone. I always needed to be with him, touching him, and reassuring him. He was very fragile and frightened. On the evenings that I attended my classes, he went over to a family member's house so as not to be alone. One particular evening while he was at a relative's house, he recognized Riana's fragrance in one of the rooms. Of course, the fragrance was only apparent to him. Frustrated, he left in torment.

Although he knew the area well, he became lost on the way home. He became disoriented. As panic set in, he called me. I could hear his fear and anxiety, which made me afraid for him. I prayed, but he was convinced he was going to die out there on the road. He kept seeing his car being broadsided by a large truck. By the time he finally made it home, he was an emotional mess. The family member that was with him that night said Paul had something very disturbing deep inside of him. Paul had some frightening anger and an extreme darkness.

The next day Paul had to return to work, and as he stopped at a red light he went into a trance and started chanting Riana's name. When he realized where he was at, he shook his head and snapped out of the trance-like state. He would later tell me that he found himself repeatedly mumbling her name for several minutes while stopped at a traffic signal. This caused fear and confusion. However, the spells seemed to come less frequently and less intense. He was getting better.

The Prayer

We both did not sleep well and I started to get hit hard by the exact oppressive spirit that would come upon Paul. I went through all of his experiences and emotions, only I was yearning for him. I had the support of family and friends who were praying and fasting on our behalf. They were warning me that these evil spirits were trying to attack and weaken me because I was the only source that was keeping Paul from going

61

insane. They confirmed what the Lord had already revealed to me.

Six days after his rescue, cutting off communication from her, it appeared Paul was less influenced by her witchcraft. He gave me explicit permission to call and check on him anytime, to monitor all his Internet activity, and to check his telephone and Email messages. He could not trust himself to be alone with Internet access, so he would unplug all the power cords from our computers and give them to me, if he had to be alone at night. He knew if he had a computer with Internet access, he would contact her. Although it appeared Paul was getting better, he still could not pray to God. He simply felt too unworthy and shameful to ask anything of God.

The seventh day after cutting all of his ties to his mistress, we had our first marriage counseling session. Paul had specific criteria for the type of counselor he would use. The counselor could not be a Christian. He did not trust them, and was quite annoyed with the entire Christian culture. He insisted he hated "church people." From the list of counselors I selected, only one replied to my inquiry. I had high hopes that this counselor would meet Paul's approval because of her "new age" philosophy. I was not disappointed.

During our counseling session, Paul related that he could not pray to God because of his shame. Therefore, the counselor suggested we pray to our dead ancestors for guidance. This exercise appealed to Paul because of his shamanistic background. As for me, I saw it as another step toward his healing.

We went outside to a large boulder on her property where there were some ancient Native American Indian petro-glyphs, and Paul was happy about this, as he loved ancient Indian rituals and magic. Our counselor lit some kind of special herb, which filled the air with fragrance and smoke. She told us to call out to our dead ancestors for help, and to pray to them to come to us and guide us in our journey to healing.

So, with the smell of sweet herbs under the shadow of an ancient boulder, with ancient Native American Indian writing on it, we called out to our dead loved ones for help. Our counselor sat on the rock, and suddenly her face transformed before our very eyes. She looked exactly like my deceased mother! Paul and I both saw this change simultaneously, and believed at the time that my dead mother had come to offer us help. We felt a release and we began to cry and pray. After some time passed, we finished the session and went home. We felt hopeful.

Now, the next event is even stranger. It occurred the following morning. As Paul drove to work, he felt very depressed. He thought he should pray to God, but he could not. Yet, the ritual from the night before had him praying to the dead, and this realization made him finally give God a try. He reasoned that if he could pray to a rock, he could pray to God.

As he was driving to work in total depression, he called out to God for help for the first time. He no longer prayed to the dead, but to the living God. As strange as it sounds, the occult ritual had broke Paul to the point where he could finally pray to God. What Satan meant for harm, God used for good. Our ways are not His ways.

That very day, Paul received a breakthrough. He began to see how his actions had hurt me and for the first time since the rescue, he apologized to me. He realized the courage that I displayed in order to confront him, and bring him home. At this moment, it was inconceivable that just a few days ago, he planned to leave our marriage for a thirteen-day affair. He was finally gaining some clarity, and this was all because he had begun to pray to God for help.

The next day, the Lord was merciful, and we had a pleasant lunch date. Although Paul was getting better, he was still tormented by dark personality shifts. Whenever the dark spirits came upon him, he became very afraid and weepy. He displayed insecurity, fear, and did not want to be alone. He felt safe when I was with him. While he slept, I stayed with him and assured him with my touch. I did homework in bed, making sure that he felt my touch while he slept. Sometimes, I would just press my foot against his foot. The Lord used these moments to draw us closer together.

When I had classes to attend at night, the Lord gave Paul a special grace and we were able to separate. However, Paul still asked me to take the computer cables and modems from the house. Even with those precautions, I firmly believed that Paul's improvements were a direct result of his prayer to God. It was a defining moment in his healing journey. I felt, if he kept this up, our marriage could heal as well.

The Battle Rages

Just when I thought Paul was getting better, he would have a relapse of sorts, and go into a deep depression with very negative thoughts. When he became depressed, he wanted to escape, give up, and return to a happier place. He blamed most of his miseries on his job. His coping skills in dealing with stress were substantially wearing away each day. Yet, there was more to Paul's drastic mood swings. There were more reasons why he could not obtain total victory in Christ.

While fasting and praying, his mother had a vision of Paul. She saw him surrounded by strong and mighty angels of God assigned to protect him from dark forces attempting to snatch his soul. However, Paul constantly was struggling with protector angels, breaking ranks, and running over to the side of his enemy. He was breaching God's protective circle. Each time Paul would break ranks, a large hand would reach out and pull him back. Paul had a similar dream where a protecting army of angels surrounded him. But, he would stick his hand through the ranks, and offer food to his enemy, who was eagerly waiting to destroy him. Why was Paul doing this? How was he feeding the enemy? What was he doing that was preventing his complete healing and deliverance?

The answer to these troubling questions rested solidly on the fact that Paul was still connected to his mistress through letters, music, gifts, and of course, thoughts. As long as he continued to listen to spellbound music, which made him sad and depressed, and as long as he continued to read letters from her, he would circumvent the mighty protection that God was supplying to him. He was having great difficulty letting go.

He tried to remove the CDs, delete her pictures, and prevent her Emails from entering his inbox. However, he would always find the music on another computer, or she would resend the pictures he had destroyed. One night, he asked his friend, Doug, to assist him in "cleaning house" at work. Late at night, they went into Paul's office, and Doug deleted every song, every picture, and every Email she sent to his computer. Doug destroyed a vase she had made, which Paul displayed in his office.

Then Doug went into Paul's car destroying everything she had given to him. This was the kind of drastic measures required in this battle. It was a form of spiritual surgery. It is important to realize that all of these objects had "attachments" on them designed to draw him to her. Spells placed on these things influenced Paul's thoughts and behavior.

In review, it was hard to imagine that all these things occurred within a two-week period! How could I sustain this fight much longer? Galatians 2:20, "I no longer live, but Christ lives in me." God was very merciful and gracious, giving me encouragement and strength.

Support Group

Two weeks to the day of his rescue, Riana contacted Paul by mail. She obviously was not going to give up without a fight. She deceitfully sent an anonymous letter to Paul. Unsuspecting Paul, who received lots of mail at his office, opened the letter and read its content. In the letter, she wrote that she had forgiven him for hurting her, and that she was moving to another place. She was willing to allow time to take its course, and assured him that he would return to her. When the time came, she would "send" for him. Her message undoubtedly scared Paul. What did she mean by "send" for him? Eerily, the letter also contained past Emails that Paul had written to her. She had "cut and pasted" them onto a sheet of paper to remind him of his promises and devotion to her. In her mind, his written promises were as a contract that he had breached, and she intended to use his words against him. He made vows that he now needed to break. He had cursed himself with these vows to her.

Paul came home and told me about the letter. Although he did not destroy it and had it in his desk, he felt sneaky keeping it from me. Again, he was having a hard time letting go of things that kept him attached to Riana. He was again depressed and wanted to quit his job, his marriage, and his life. There would be a pattern emerging. Every time he heard or saw something from this woman, his character would become weak.

67

However, the longer he would stay away from the music she had sent him, or refrain from reading her Emails and letters, his character would become stronger. The spell would loosen its stronghold with no contact. Remember, everything she sent him had a demonic "attachment" on it.

Paul needed a support group at work to assist him as I was assisting him at home. He had Doug, a friend that he confided in, and Doug was always holding Paul accountable. He is the one that "cleaned house" at Paul's office when Paul returned to work after the rescue. Now God was going to give Paul another helper, and this lady was instrumental in opening Paul's eyes to the severity of the witchcraft that was plaguing him. I will refer to her as Maria.

Maria was one of Paul's civilian support staff under his command. She was a quiet professional who knew Paul but was not close to him personally. Maria told Paul on two occasions, "You look sad." She saw a great sadness in his eyes and just mentioned it to him. Paul felt compelled to talk to her about his situation. He reasoned that because Maria was Hispanic (like him), and often Hispanics are more culturally in tune with the supernatural, spirits, witchcraft and hexes, she may know how to break the curse that was on him.

Paul called Maria into his office and asked her if she believed in "love spells" and other hexes. She affirmed that she did believe and that love spells were very common in her culture. She related that her own brother was under a spell and turned into a zombie-like man who was used and manipulated by his lover. Then Paul told her everything that had happened so far. After patiently listening, she had no doubt that Paul was hexed. This explained why he had looked so sad to her recently.

Maria began to shed light on things. She asked Paul a hypothetical question, "If this other woman were to come to your house and fight with Linda, who would you defend?" Paul said, "My wife." Maria replied, "There is no difference in defending Linda's emotions. This other woman is a thief. She wants to steal your love, not earn it. She wants to steal your money and position. She is the lowest of the lowest." Maria cautioned Paul, "This woman is dangerous. If she cannot have you, then no one will. That is why you have thoughts of suicide, not wanting to live, and have hopelessness. She is using magic to manipulate and deceive you."

Paul told Maria about the letter he just received and how he felt sneaky reading and concealing it. Maria told him that he must confess it to me. "She is trying to create a wedge between you and your wife. This is what she is intending." Keeping secrets from your spouse is a red flag something may be wrong within your relationship.

Maria gave Paul a stern warning about possessing anything from this other woman. She told him that he must cut off all ties and communication, no exceptions. Paul asked Maria, "How do I break the spell?" She said, "Paul, you must connect to God. It can't fight against true love." Maria told Paul what everyone else had been telling him, disconnect completely from this woman or be burned.

An interesting insight occurred when Maria told Paul that this woman intends to destroy him now that he is fighting against her. I was also experiencing thoughts of suicide, hopelessness, and feelings of imminent death. I had imaginations that I would be involved in a fatal car crash, and then Paul would be released to return to her. These images would make me fearful, until I rebuked those thoughts in the authority of Jesus my Lord.

Paul asked Maria to assist him by sorting his mail. They set up a support group at his office. She would review his mail, before giving it to him, and if she saw a suspicious package she would open it, verify if it was from Riana, and then shred it. She also assisted him in blocking Emails that came from her. Between Maria and Doug, they were able to keep Paul clear of any influences sent to him. Paul was trying to do everything right to combat this evil.

Demons in Our Bedroom

I awakened at 3:00 or 4:00 AM every night for a week, and I would pray for Paul at this hour. Two weeks and two days after the rescue, I woke up at 4:00 AM and looked at Paul who was asleep, but something was not right. God impressed upon me to place my hands on his head and pray. Later that morning, he told me that he had heard chanting in his sleep again. He heard the voice of his jilted lover repeating a rhyme in his mind. The voice was telling him that he belonged to her. However, in his unconscious state, he told the voice, "No way!" Suddenly, his mind became alert and he knew that he had to remember this incident. Now I knew why God had prompted me to place my hands on Paul's head and pray.

Paul realized that this voice and rhyme had been coming to him in his sleep all week. He remembered that this Wiccan woman was up in the dark hours of the night, and that is when she would do her magic. It seemed she was now getting frustrated with me for blocking access to Paul, and was literally inserting herself into his dreams at night. But, it gets worse.

The next night, I awoke at 4:00 AM again, but this time the room was wildly spinning. I had double vision, and I could not shake the spinning and accompanied nausea. I got up and played a Christian music CD and tried to go back to sleep. Paul heard me moaning and woke me up. He also had a dream that he was trapped in a small box and could not get out.

When I told him about the spinning room, he decided to get up but he could not see because of the intense "fog" in our bedroom. He stumbled around and put on his glasses to see. He finally got up and left the room, and when he returned, the fog was gone. This was the beginning of seeing and feeling this demonic "fog" come into our room. It resembled real fog or smoke, and blurred the vision. It was always accompanied with an evil presence.

71

After we prayed, we both went back to sleep, but I heard him "agreeing" to something in his sleep. I quickly said, "No!" and began to pray fervently. At the very exact hour, Paul's sister was awakened and impressed to pray for us. I thanked God for this kind of support because these events were becoming stranger as the days went on. And now, like an animal being stalked by a hunter, Paul and I were about to face some of the most powerful magic yet. Because of the fine details and experiences with emotion, Paul will continue telling our story from his perspective.

Chapter 4: The Hunted

Soul Ties

I (Paul) was getting stronger the more I removed myself from any demonic influence. I had to absolutely stop listening to her music, reading her Emails or letters. I had to destroy every piece of pottery or gift Riana had given me. I cannot begin to explain the intense draw these items had on me.

My support group was set up at work and at home, and so I was protected and isolated from harm. The more I heeded to sound advice and prayed to God for help, the stronger I became. I started to renew my marriage and repair my sick psyche.

There was a definite pattern. If I had any - I mean the slightest - contact with Riana, I would become depressed and demonized. My whole character would change and I would become one of many different personalities. The most often persona manifested was this whiny, sobbing, negative, depressed little pathetic character Linda had nicknamed "Paulina" because it acted like a little spoiled girl. When this demon would attach to my psyche, thoughts of suicide or certain death would envelope me. "Paulina" brought pure hopelessness with her. I can only imagine this is what suicide victims feel, before taking their own lives.

I also manifested another persona that was much more hateful and cruel. This persona was dangerous and others could "feel" the intense anger emanating from me. I can only imagine this is what a murderer feels before taking the life of another.

Was I demon possessed? No. Yet, I was demon oppressed with demonically controlled emotions and thoughts. My spirit was not strong enough to combat them, and so I would yield to their influence. Although, I was beginning to act and talk like my old self with a renewed love and interest for my wife, something sinister was about to unfold.

It was a day shy of being three weeks since the day of my rescue. That morning, my sister and my mother were both awakened at 2:30 AM and were impressed to pray for us. For the last three weeks, this had been almost a nightly occurrence among family members. Additionally, it seemed that God had given Linda a sort of radar or warning device before danger. She would get pangs or aches in her stomach before any demonic activity. Her stomach pangs were a reliable tool to discern trouble. On this particular morning, Linda's stomach was hurting, she was depressed, nervous, and dizzy. Thoughts of killing herself flowed in and out of her mind. Something was very wrong.

The Surprise Visit

I drove to work as usual, feeling stronger and more alive than ever. I parked in my assigned parking space in front of the police station. I was looking down gathering my briefcase when suddenly "she" was there standing right outside my driver's side window! Riana had hunted me down, stalked her prey, and was now suddenly pouncing on it.

I opened my door and said, "What are you doing here?" She looked at me intently and said, "I can see in your face that I lost you. You look different." She immediately turned around and started to walk away. She obviously could see the spell broke by the look on my face. I thought to myself now would be the time to put an end to all of this nonsense. And, why not? I was feeling much stronger, and no longer felt a supernatural draw towards her. This was a bad mistake on my part. I should have just allowed her to walk away.

I called out to her and suggested that we go get some coffee and talk about what had happened. So, we went to a local coffee shop, and there I asked her if she had placed a spell on me. She denied it while grinning, but suggested I place "salt" under my pillow to keep the demons away. She also gave me her pocketknife, and told me that it was silver to protect me from evil. She ordered me to never let it out of my sight. I took the knife. As soon as I got back to the police station, I threw it into a deep trash receptacle.

Additionally, she handed me another package. In this envelope were several white "sachet bags" to place salt or herbs into, a fan made out of crow feathers, and a book of philosophy. I also gave this package to my support group to destroy in my behalf.

While drinking coffee with her, I was afraid and did not trust her at all. I was nice but firm. I told her that I loved my wife, and would stay with my marriage. She cried, saying she only wanted me to be happy, and so "released" me. It seemed it was all over now. No more demons at night, no more fog in our bedroom, and no more waking up in the middle of the night with strange voices and dreams in my head.

We ended up on a cordial note, and I felt really strong and good about my behavior and actions. I knew that I had come a long way in three weeks. I knew that had she come to visit earlier, I would have succumbed to the magic. I called Linda to tell her what had happened. Her stomach pains had already warned her of the danger. But, this time was different I said. I am stronger and unaffected by this woman.

Linda and I talked about the visit when I returned home from work. We both were hopeful that the crazy ride we were on was about to stop. Yet, Linda was still experiencing pain in her stomach, so we both agreed we had to be alert and cautious. Riana did not seem to be the type to let go easily. This should have been the end of my hex and the end of this book, but it was not.

Dream Magic

The next day, I was messed up in the head. I went from being a strong man standing his ground to a weak, depressed, sniveling little baby. "Paulina" was back in full force. Why could I not get complete deliverance from this spell? I had a wonderful Christian wife who was constantly praying, I had family that was constantly fasting and praying for me, and I had a loving support

76

group all around me. What was wrong? What was I doing wrong? The answer was in the contact. As Linda had pointed out, although I did not keep any of Riana's gifts, I had accepted them, and it was enough to send me back to my tormenting prison.

That night the bad dreams started. Dreams projected like a movie. Dreams like impressions coming from the outside of my mind. I would see all the accruements of witchcraft used on me. They were weird and frightening dreams, and at the same time encouraged my fascination with the occult.

While asleep, I saw a mirror and received impressions that I belonged to Riana, and would return to her. I also saw Maria from my support group, and knew she was in trouble. This would turn out to be true within a matter of weeks. Additionally, I saw a white cord with a knot tied at the top. I awoke suddenly and knew the images were of witchcraft, but did not understand exactly what they meant. I looked at the clock; it was 2:05 AM. Then I smelled the strong aroma of freshly brewed coffee - I mean delicious smelling coffee, and then had distinct words come to me. They said, "Wake up and smell the coffee." Immediately my memory flashed back to the day before when I last had coffee with Riana.

This was the second time I had heard affirmations in my sleep that said, "You will be mine and you will come back to me." I felt my subconscious mind fighting the affirmations, and waking me up. So many strange things were happening accompanied with constant depression and sadness.

The next day, Linda and I discussed what had happened to me in the night. We decided not to dwell on the occult side of things too much, after researching spells on the Internet. We found that a white cord or string used in a love spell will have a knot tied to seal and bring back a lover. If the knot is untied, a release of a lover is signified. In my sleep, I saw a white cord with a tied knot on it. Later that day while Linda and I were getting out of my car, I smelled the "sandalwood fragrance of Riana. I feverishly started sniffing my arms and hands to locate where the smell was coming from. It was real and I instinctively knew Riana was not letting go.

That night as I slept, I could hear the barn owls living above our bedroom making a lot of noise, they were hissing and banging about. I had dream impressions again, and I thought that the owls were giving me the interpretation of the impressions. I saw a black ladder and black and red cords. Suddenly, my subconscious mind awoke me in a frightened panic. The clock read, 2:05 AM again.

In the morning, I told Linda about the impressions but could not remember the interpretations. We both felt that Satan was bringing these intrusions into our lives to take our focus from God. This was true as the nightly torment was draining both of us physically and emotionally. I was becoming too tired to fight. Like clockwork, that night we both awoke again at 2:05 AM, but could not recall any dreams or impressions.

The Bewitching Hour

Ever since Riana's "surprise visit," things had gotten worse for me. I was plagued with weird dreams, occurrences, and depression. Confusion was now my constant companion. Linda believed that I had given Riana too much information about us, and now she was changing her strategy to first separate our marriage and then lure me back with spell binding.

There is a room in our house, which Linda's now deceased mother used to sleep in when she stayed with us. We called this room, "Mama's room," and now Linda uses this room to pray and study her Bible and educational studies. This room is special to Linda. Once again at 2:05 AM, Linda suddenly awoke, but I stayed asleep. In the morning, I told her about a dream I had. I dreamed that Riana was in "Mama's room" on the bed laughing. In my dream, I knew that this would make Linda angry. The enemy's strategy was certainly attempting to get Linda angry, unforgiving, and weak. That way, this woman could separate us and then work her magic to conquer me.

With the bewitching hour always at 2:05 AM, I became agitated. Our eyes would just suddenly pop open and we would both be awake and alert. We would look at the clocks and always they would read 2:05 AM. My depression started to deepen. I felt distant from Linda and missed the "happy times" I used to have when I was with Riana. I did not miss her, but the "experience" of being free and peaceful. I knew that I would not feel that way again unless I was with Riana. I was like a moth drawn to a flame, flying wildly to my certain death. I was so confused because the feelings I had seemed real, but I knew they were not rooted in reality. I could not discern between what was real and what was magic. Everything I saw was a sign to me from her. I thought she was trying to contact me through dreams and other occurrences.

Riana told me once that her spirit animal was the "raven," and called by that name as a child. In my spiritual funk and confusion, I walked out my front door and found a beautiful and perfect raven feather perched just right at the threshold. I took this as a sign Riana contacted me. This never happened again. I felt she was thinking of me and I of her. I was hitting rock bottom, and I told Linda that I felt guilty for putting her through all of this. I felt very lost and sad with thoughts of just giving up and returning to Riana.

It had been exactly one week since Riana's surprise visit, and I was deeply troubled. Satan was telling me all sorts of lies about my weakness and depression. Yet, I could not even remember that I was strong and on my way to a healing marriage before Riana's visit. That last contact really was harmful. It was one of the worst mistakes I had made in this situation. Unfortunately, it would not be my last.

I felt hands on my back, which startled me. It was 2:35 AM, and I asked Linda if she had touched me; she had.

She was praying over me. I remembered that before her touch, I saw in my mind a picture of Riana from a photograph she had. Words flashed across my mind, which read I belonged to her and would return. The image and the words instantly disappeared when Linda placed her hands on my back and started to pray to God over my soul. Yet, I was still in a deep dark fog mentally and emotionally.

I finally hit the bottom of the pit of Hell. I told Linda the grief and sadness in my heart was unbearable, and that I must return to Riana. I knew that I would be sealing my doom, but felt I could not resist her calling any longer. I told my wife that I loved her very much and could not keep putting her through all this weirdness. It is so hard to explain, but I had honestly believed that facing my certain doom with Riana was my destiny. My heart ached and I felt loss and grief at an intensity like never before. I was going to return, just as the words in my dreams repeatedly commanded me to do.

Now Linda could see that I was under a deep delusion. My "supposed" deep grief and sorrow just started manifesting that day. Yet to me, it seemed like I had always felt this way, and I could not remember being strong. Linda reminded me that a week before Riana contacted me, I was strong and was healing. She reminded me that I was under a strong delusion. I could hardly believe her when she told me that it had only been a week since Riana's last contact. In my mind, I thought I had been depressed for weeks. The spell caused distortions of time. Through all of this, God reassured Linda everything was going to be fine and the magic was not going to stick. She had to hold onto these promises of God.

Linda begged me to give her just one more week before returning to Riana because she knew I was not thinking correctly. Linda knew that I was buying into a lie from Hell. I agreed, but I was very afraid that I was going to do something stupid. I was at the bottom of this pit hanging on by a thread.

It is important to note that while I was beginning to pray to God for help, I only wanted the torment to leave me and return to "normal." My prayers to God were egocentric and self-centered. They were all about "me" finding relief from this demonic love spell.
Additionally, I was still very much into occult beliefs and magic. I was confused and dulled. I wanted to seek an "herbalist" in an attempt to cure me. I thought of seeking a "healer" (witch) to break the spell on me. That is how confused I was. The confusion was like a shadow that would engulf me causing mental dullness.

Chapter 5: The Repentance

Demon of Suicide

Four weeks prior, Linda had physically brought me home and rescued me from a witch. It was exactly fours weeks to the day when we had a very bad night. It was a typical night of terror and torment, being awakened at 2:05AM, feeling an evil presence, and seeing a thick fog in our bedroom. It was a typical night of strange and unremembered dreams, demonic groans, and crying. The "audio Bible" we had constantly playing in our room would garble and warble, making the verses unintelligible. We would lie there awake and pray for the morning light. The fatigue and mental stress was becoming unbearable for both of us. It was sheer torment.

On my way to work the next morning, I received a message from my mother who said, "Paul, Satan is a liar and the father of all lies. He is a deceiver and he came to rob, steal and destroy. You cannot trust or believe him, ever. He is not your friend and he does not love you." I could sense my mother's anger at Satan, and I wished badly that I could just get mad again. I wished that I could get angry with Satan and authoritatively cast him away through the authority of Christ. But, I could not.

I was too weak, too sinful, too unworthy, too sad, and too depressed to do anything about my torment. I knew what I needed. I needed to get angry with my enemy and fight back. But, I was a coward, and instead asked my mother to use her anger to curse the demons from me. What I did not realize was that God heard my "wish" and something was about to get me angry, very angry. This would make a difference in the battle.

By noon, I was eating lunch with Doug. I was spilling out all of my depression, sadness, and hopelessness on him. I told him how I wanted to give up and just return to the witch, knowing that I was going to my destruction. I could not fight it any longer. Doug looked cautiously at me and said, "Paul, you have tried everything but I honestly have not seen you commit to God or to a place of worship." He continued, "You need to ask yourself, what is God trying to tell me?" His words cut like a sword. He was right.

I had "somewhat" prayed to God several weeks ago after my first therapy session when I could only pray to a rock. I had talked to God while driving to and from work, asking Him to remove my torment. However, I had not repented. I had not asked God for mercy and grace. I had not asked God to forgive my sins and to cleanse me. I had not invited the blood of Christ to repair my torn and wounded soul.

At the same time, Linda was at home reading a book on spiritual warfare, and she read something that discouraged her. She read that I had to repent and ask forgiveness in order to close the open demonic door. Until I repented, the door allowing this torment would remain open and the harassment would continue. Linda began to pray that God would bring healing to my spirit.

She knew that I had to sincerely repent before God. How was I going to get to that place? Then Linda's sister, Patty called. During the conversation, Patty told her, "Listen, Paul has to repent of his sins before God, if he wants this torment to stop." All of these messages were loud and clear, "repent and stop sinning."

A few hours later, Linda was at home alone in our study doing some research for one of her classes when she began to notice her stomach pangs warning her of danger. Then dark fog entered the room. As she was typing her paper, she noticed the screen seemed hazy. She stopped typing and examined the letters on the screen, but her vision became distorted with each blink of the eye. She looked up and noticed a fog was developing in the room. Familiar with this phenomenon, she went into alert mode.

Immediately, she sensed an evil presence in the room. Its presence was so invasive that she turned around expecting to see a physical being, but the only thing she saw was the open door that led out into the hallway. She sensed that the evil spirit was encroaching closer to her. Her heart started to pound within her and fear was banging to enter. At once, the Lord impressed upon her to call for reinforcement. I was her first call, but I was unavailable. She left a message saying that an evil presence was in the room and she needed prayer. Her second call was to my mom, but no answer. She left her a similar message. Her last call was to Patty and again no answer. The evil presence was upon her. Her heart was racing and she knew she needed help. She prayed a quick, "Jesus, help me."

She managed to type a short email to me as the evil spirit fell upon her like a heavy cloak. It was suffocating and she felt her body begin to hunch forward involuntarily. Her shoulders rolling inward, her head began to lower, and her eyes were closing. She felt this immense emotional pain deep inside her soul. She said it felt like her soul plummeted into a dark abyss where it felt very dark and isolated. She felt as if she was alone with no hope. The pain was so intense that she began to wail; not cry, but wail from deep inside.

At the same time, she heard a female voice whispering in her head telling her that she needed to kill herself. She was unworthy to live. She received images of herself hanging from the ceiling; just dangling there. The voice urged her to kill herself so I would find her dead body. Linda said that the suggestions and the feelings were incredibly strong. She felt as if she were in a trance, and wanted to obey the fiendish suggestion to take her life, but at the same time, her mind was clear. The suggestions were coming from the outside to her mind, and not from within herself. These thoughts were not her thoughts; therefore, her mind was "clear."

She was unable to stop wailing and crying uncontrollable sobs. The evil spirit was able to control her body, but her mind or spirit was untouchable. She had clarity of thought. She knew she did not want to commit suicide, but she was unable to stop the physical and emotional developments. It was not long after she hit the send button to my email, when Patty called. Linda answered the phone in sobs. She did not want Patty to be overly alarmed so she explained that she sounded worse than it appeared. She told Patty about the strong urge to commit suicide, but she knew in her mind that she did not want to do it. Patty told her she needed to get out of that room.

Linda explained through her sobs that she could not move. The evil spirit was like a heavy weight on her body and her breathing was shallow. Patty said she would stay on the phone with her. Linda used her right foot to turn the swivel chair around to face the door. Time appeared to be in slow motion. The thought of rising from the chair seemed an impossible feat. Once again, Linda prayed, "Jesus, help me." Just then, our English Mastiff wandered into the room. The large dog approached Linda, who was then able to use it as a crutch to exit the room. As Linda stood, she found it interesting that she was unable to straighten her torso. She remained in a hunched posture with her head lowered, and her eyelids half shut.

She continued to hear the whispers, and the images of her body hanging from the ceiling would pulsate in and out of her mind. She managed to slowly stumble out of the room through the living room and out the front door. Patty remained on the phone with her the entire time. Patty warned, "Paul must repent. If he does not repent, then this kind of stuff will continue to happen. He has left an open door, which puts you in danger." Linda said she reached the porch exhausted and was glad to find the comfort of the rocking chair. At that moment, Linda received my call. I told her to hold on because I was on my way home.

The Anger

Now, I became angry. This demonic attack on my wife trying to lead her into suicide was the catalyst I needed to become really angry with Satan and his tormentors. Realizing that I had no one to fight the enemy on my behalf, I knew I had to do battle. I was the one who had to get serious about stopping this torment. I raced home.

What would I do? I looked up to the sky and said to God, "If you are really an all powerful God, and have more power than these evil spirits, then show yourself to me. Please God, reveal yourself." And it was then that somehow - I do not know how- that I knew my God was absolutely and unequivocally more powerful. I cried out, "What do I need to do?" The Lord said, "Take authority over evil through the Holy Divine Blood of my Son the Lord Jesus Christ. Claim your redemption for I am the God of wonders beyond the galaxy, Lord of all creation, and I am holy."

When I arrived home, Linda was outside huddled in a ball in a chair. She was not even aware of my presence. Her eyes were glassy and had a far away look to them. Her body was immobile and she could not move. She looked like a person who had ingested extreme drugs - some type of central nervous system depressant. Linda was sobbing uncontrollably, like a person gone insane. I knew she was under the influence of something very evil and sinister.

I took her hand and said, "Linda, I need you to believe right now because where there are two or more people gathered together in the Lord's name, He will be there also." I had no idea what I was doing, but simply had to follow whatever popped into my head. I had prayed to God for guidance, and now I had to accept that the thoughts in my mind were from God.

I took a Bible, and opened it to the Psalms. I do not know why I picked the Psalms, but they were the Scriptures I wanted to find. The pages landed on Psalm 91, and so Psalm 91 it was. I placed the Bible in Linda's hands and had her read Psalm 91 aloud repeatedly. I gathered some Christian praise music and blasted it in the background, and then I beseeched God to intervene in our behalf.

Linda began to read aloud, "He who dwells in the shelter of the most high will abide in the shadow of the Almighty. I will say to the LORD, 'My refuge and my fortress, my God, in whom I trust!'" I did what God had told me to do, take authority over this evil spirit in the name of Jesus Christ my Lord. After praying fervently, the evil spirit that had descended on Linda left her. Her eyes returned to normal, as well as, her personality. We held each other tightly. I knew the evil presence had to be removed through the authority of Christ regardless of my own pitiful sinner state. Christ did the work. It was then I realized the power of salvation. It was a free gift to me, and I was not deserving of it in any way.

As we prayed and thanked God for His deliverance in battle, Linda began to pray and speak authoritatively from God. She slammed the palm of her hand against my chest and yelled, "Paul, your God has delivered you today! You belong to me (God). Your life is not yours to give away." Something powerful rushed through my core and I fell onto my knees weeping before God. I cried out, "God, forgive me! Wash me in the blood of Jesus, and remove my sins! I repent of my rebellion against you. Please return your grace into my life."

For the first time in four weeks since Linda rescued me, I truly understood the gravity of my sin, and this time when I told her I was sorry for what I did, I really meant it. I apologized to her, and asked forgiveness. For the first time in four weeks, I repented of my sin and asked God to renew my spirit. I had entrenched myself into God's wonder and mercy for the first time in years. It was wonderful. He was the warrior God of the Old Testament, as well as, the God of grace in the New Testament.

However, I had no idea of the journey that was to begin. I had to learn everything about spiritual battle, but at this point, I thought the torment was all over, and life would resume like before. I was so wrong. Our enemy stepped up his attack strategy.

The same night that I repented of my sins and discovered true victory, Linda and I were awakened again at 2:05 AM, and we saw that same familiar "fog" accompanied by an evil presence in our bedroom. Linda looked over at me, and I was awake, but this time I was smiling. As Linda prayed in the Spirit of Christ, I took my Bible, opened it up to Psalm 27, and began to read aloud. I began to remove this evil from our room through the power of Christ our Lord. The fog left. The evil presence was gone. We both felt Riana would continue trying to contact me, but this time there would be no "open door" for her magic to take affect on us. We fell into a deep sleep, and the Holy Spirit ministered to me, and gave me sermons in my sleep.

The next night, we both awakened at 1:55 AM and were dreading the 2:05 AM bewitching hour. But then, we realized nothing was going to happen, and we returned to peaceful sleep. We slept past the 2:05 AM hour without incident. Far away in another city, my younger sister awoke at 1:15 AM, and began to pray for us. At 1:57 AM she said aloud, "It's all gone." We took this as a confirmation that the enemy lost his stronghold on us. Yet, as Linda so aptly put it, "We are like victims of a car crash trying to adjust to driving again." We knew we had to work through our fears, communicate with each other, and trust in God.

A few days later, while asleep, I felt breath on my back, and I asked Linda if she had done it. She did not. At the same time this occurred, I heard a voice in my dreams, which I thought was an angel voice. It said, "A battle is being fought over you, Paul, and the battle is in Heaven." At the time, I was disappointed with that news because I thought the whole torment thing was over and done. I did not want to hear that a battle was still being fought over me. I had no idea about spiritual warfare at the time.

Linda reminded me that it was a good message, and that we needed to stay alert and ready for battle. She told me I was delivered, and the portal closed. The evil could not come through the closed door. I certainly had no doubts God delivered me. I had repented of my sins and asked God and Linda to forgive me. However, I still only wanted the demonic torment to stop, and had little idea that the Christian walk would be hard and difficult at times. I did not realize the narrow gate before me. I just wanted to be normal again. At this time, it was important to realize that the demonic attacks were just that – attacks from the enemy, and not caused by an open door related to my sin. That is why there was no depression or sadness anymore.

It was nice for us to get some sleep, as we were so tired and worn out. Linda and I were finally sleeping through the 2:05 AM bewitching hour, but my sisters and mother were not. They awoke at this hour, and continually urged to pray for us. I was still having dreams that I could not remember upon waking, but I felt Riana still attempting incantations to draw me back to her. But, it was a nice transition period for two battle worn people.

Our support group awoke at the bewitching hour experiencing strange occurrences. In one night, an extreme invasion of demonic forces transcended city and state lines to execute an assault of fear and torment on anyone who was supporting us.

This demonic assault occurred about five weeks after my rescue and one week since my repentance and deliverance. On this particular night, my eldest sister had a demonic visitation while she slept. This evil spirit harassed and bothered her with fear for most of the night until she eventually got angry enough to remove it in the authority of Christ.

During the same night, far off in another city, my youngest sister awoke to an extreme evil presence in her bedroom. This thing kept her awake with fear for the majority of the night. She also finally overcame it through the authority of Christ.

While my sisters fought their demons, my niece living in another state had her own encounter with an evil presence. While she slept, a dark shadow hovered over her, and she became highly frightened. She eventually came against the thing in the name of Jesus, and it left her.

That very night, I felt a strong evil presence in our bedroom. I smelled something burning. Linda also smelled it. I can only describe it as a mixture of flesh and dirt. The evil was a heavy dark shadow pressing against my face, and I was afraid. It felt like it was trying to enter my body.

I also felt I needed to learn to engage in spiritual warfare, and not rely on others to do it for me. I prayed, but the spirit would not go away. Then I remembered what the angel voice had told me, "There is a heavenly battle being fought over you." I continued to pray, and realized that just as Moses had to lift up his hands as Joshua and his warriors fought, or the battle would be lost (Exodus 17:8-13), I would have to continue to walk with God and lift prayers up in order for this evil to stop its harassment. It was one of my first lessons in learning how to fight in another realm. Perseverance was key.

The next morning, my mother was at a car wash. She sat outside while reading a book when she smelled a strong "woody" burning odor surrounding her. Through the corner of her eye, she saw small puffs of smoke around her. She thought maybe there was a lit cigarette inside one of the trash receptacles. She called an employee to investigate. He found nothing. She began to sense this was supernatural, which prompted her to pray.

This concerted spiritual attack on our support group was not limited to family members. My friend Maria did not show up at work. She had a dark demonic presence come over her, and it caused her to become very sick with vertigo and nausea. She became so sick that she could not get out of her bed. This very dizziness would soon become a common method of attack for Linda and me.

That morning, everyone was Emailing Linda and telling her of their strange visitations and invasion of evil. She started connecting the dots, and discovered the attacks were an all out assault on our support group. It seemed this evil curse was now harassing all of our prayer and support partners. Disembodied spirits were now visiting anyone close to us. As for us, the early morning awakenings accompanied with strange dreams and weird smells would continue to be a nightly occurrence.

Going Back to the Hotel

Six weeks since my day of rescue, I had to return to the city where I committed adultery. My job was sending me there to complete a project, and I was very concerned because of the past. Linda decided to go with me, and we prayed for God's help. We were to stay at the same hotel that I stayed at with Riana. We went and spent the week in this city, and had some leisure time in between my work project. My biggest concern was avoiding depression. I did not want to do anything, which would open the doors to the demonic. I had had a real experience with God a few weeks prior – an experience of salvation that I had not felt since I was first saved at age fifteen. I certainly did not want to go back into that dark life of sin.

It was a strange week for sure with a few spiritual attacks, which was no surprise. Many places Linda and I went reminded me of what I did just six weeks prior. There were many mixed and ugly feelings. There were also some strange happenings and things that were out of the ordinary.

Linda and I went to a movie theater enjoying the film when I suddenly started experiencing an extreme unbearable heat throughout my body. I was getting hotter by the second. It was very unnatural. I told Linda that the heat was becoming excruciating. A strong survival urge came over me. I needed to rip my shirt from my body, and run out of the theater and try to get into the night air. Resisting the impulse to run, but unbuttoning my shirt, the heat finally subsided. I had never experienced anything like that since that time. It was an internal demonic heat.

During the trip, we went to a bookstore to browse around. Something odd happened to me. I walked into the store, and immediately went to the occult / witchcraft section. There I stood in front of the books of magic, spells, and incantations. I was fascinated with them, and had a strong desire to know the magic they contained. Linda was in another section, and decided to find me. Well, she did find me, just staring at the occult books. She asked me what I was doing, and I told her that I needed to know what had happened to me. I needed to know what kind of spell and magic Riana used on me. I was in a trance.

Linda immediately told me that I knew as much as I needed to know, and then she pulled me away from those books. Understand this is how I got involved with the occult through my curiosity with power. These books on witchcraft and magic would absolutely be an open door for demons to return into my life.

Now the week was over and we made it. No devastating incidents occurred and we were both closer to one another. The Holy Spirit was growing me in truth, and I was becoming stronger and closer to God. Linda was experiencing new heights in her relationship with the Creator God. However, we were not out of the woods yet. The enemy of our marriage was still trying every conceivable deception to get me side-tracked.

The Haunting

The first night back in our house, Linda woke up again at that bewitching hour of 2:05 AM, and then fell back asleep only to reawaken at 3:30 AM with a fierce evil presence in our bedroom. She felt that something bad was happening to me in my sleep. In the morning, I told her I was fine, but she was suspicious. She discerned that I was not right. We would soon learn that evil spirits loved to visit us in the night hours as our conscious self gave way to our subconscious. They would whisper and place ideas and thoughts in our heads so that upon waking we would be under the influence of their hypnosis. It was imperative to ask for God's protection during the night, but I had not arrived at that lesson yet.

That morning I had a dentist appointment. While driving to the office, I had an overwhelming desire to telephone Riana. The impulse was near uncontrollable, like an unseen force driving me to my destruction. An overwhelming sadness engulfed me once again, and I thought that the only way to get relief was to call Riana. However, in my rational mind, I knew this to be a lie. During those times, the thoughts would overcome me because they seemed so real. Linda and I had made great positive strides in recent weeks, and now this strange impulse was pushing me to a place I did not want to return. The urge left me as I arrived at my appointment. However, the events just became worse, when an enchanted song began to play.

The music Riana sent me had spells on it. I could not listen to any of the songs associated with her without becoming depressed, and emotionally swept away to a dark place. The music was my "Kryptonite" so to speak. If some of the music started to play in a public place, I would have to literally excuse myself and leave the room in order to remove my spirit from the enchanted song. This was easier with Linda, but very difficult when I was eating lunch with co-workers. I would use a telephone call or go to the restroom as an excuse to leave the room. People would not understand.

Going into the seventh week since my rescue date, I found myself literally confined to a dentist's chair surrounded by the dentist and his technicians. With my mouth wide open filled with dental devices, I began to hear a particular love song over the office speakers. This song was a special song because I had dreamed it in a night vision of her the first week we met. It became "our song." Of all the magical music affecting me, this had to be the most potent. I absolutely could not subject myself to hear it without spinning into a deep depression. Additionally, I had just fought off the incredible urge to call her. But, I could not move, could not excuse myself and leave, or explain my danger to the doctor and his staff.

I sat there and listened to the music with tears streaming down my face. It was a cruel torture, but then again, I had cruel tormentors. At this point, I was really trying to learn and walk with God, be a deserving husband, and change my ways. I was fought every step of the way. Whatever had its hold on me would not easily let go.

Meanwhile at home, Linda sensed something was terribly wrong, so she prayed. When I returned home, I told her of everything that had happened to me. There were to be no secrets between us anymore. Now it made sense to her why she was feeling something was wrong with me. We were also learning to trust Linda's "gut" instinct as a warning from God about impending danger. The Lord would give us both little tools to use to assist us in combating these deceiving spirits. After, I told Linda about the demonic attack against me the sadness and depression left.

Then that night I woke up to Linda's jerking around in her sleep. The clock read 2:05 AM. I could hardly see inside the room because the demonic fog had returned. After waking Linda, we prayed and fell back asleep. Although we still sensed a very evil presence in our room, we knew God's angelic army was shielding us. It was becoming clear that we needed some Spirit-filled Christians to assist us in cleansing our house.

I knew in my heart that I needed a Spirit-filled man to lay hands on me and pray over me. This was unusual for me because I normally would not be around anyone who would do such a thing. Yet, I just "instinctively" knew that this is what I needed. It felt like our house was haunted, but in reality it was me that was haunted. At the time, I did not know about God's order in marriage. The man, who is the priest of his house, always "covers" his wife and household. Christ then covers the man just as He covers the church. So, as long as I refused to take on my priestly duty as God's man of our house and cover my wife, as Christ covers His church, she would be adversely affected by my behavior (Ephesians 5:22-33).

Chapter 6: The Dark Return to Hell

Finding Value in the Suffering

We wish we did not have to write this portion of the book. It is a horrid and shameful experience for a man to return to his vomit. Yet, it happened, and it was bad. The lesson to learn is that Satan, the enemy of your marriage, roams around like a roaring lion seeking someone he can devour. Because of this, we must always entertain a sober spirit and be alert to our enemy (1Peter 5:8).

Perhaps it was complacency or over confidence, that caused the reconnect to Riana. May be it was the skillful deception of evil spirits that still claimed my soul. More than likely, it was my lack of self-discipline. In any case, the end-result was sin. A rebellion against God's commands leading to a near fatal ending was the outcome of pure unabashed sin. Fortunately, the re-contact only lasted about two weeks, but the resulting torment would increase to unbearable proportions during the next month. There was a cause and an effect, and a high price to pay for my indiscretion and disobedience. We would both pay a high price for that cause.

I (Paul) realized that my enemy was fighting hard, and that it would take time to walk in God's wisdom. I began reading a book on spiritual warfare and it was making sense to me. I started to understand some of the tactics of Satan. Although, still being attacked with

101

various demonic emotions, I was not under the influence of demons anymore. I was getting stronger in God. Yet, I would still have thoughts, "What is she doing right now?" or "Is she thinking of me?" I would recognize the thoughts as a new tactic from the enemy trying to get into my head. I would know they were lies and refute them. Linda said that I was leaning to tear down strongholds and imaginations.

The major lesson for me was to submit to God's authority, and then I would be protected. Remember, for years, I did not submit to anyone or anything, so this was new to me. Everything I read, watched, and heard had this theme running through it, "Submit to God." It was painful, but I was learning and seeing a positive side to the suffering as well.

All this suffering was bringing a huge benefit; we were both learning spiritual discernment. We could recognize demonic strongholds in the lives of other people. We noticed that our perspectives were changing. Things that once seemed innocuous were now viewed in the spiritual light. For example, we discussed how women obsessed with romantic novels were missing romance and intimacy in their lives. It is when they lust after the character or covet the theme in the story that they cross the spiritual threshold and create a space for demonic influences in their minds. We were learning to see the subtle craftiness of Satan, and to recognize the various spiritual strongholds that bonded people to evil and destruction, even good Christian people.

There is a big difference in the testing of the Lord to build up spiritual character, and the suffering caused by one's own sin. I had experienced both, so what I did next was unfathomable.

A Birthday Gift

I was still having strange thoughts come into my mind regarding Riana. I had not learned to combat these thoughts, and I did not discover how much the war zone is contained in the mind. You would think it would be obvious by now, but it took me awhile to understand that Satan can only deceive you through your thoughts (2Corinthians 10:5). These thoughts then become actions and behaviors, illnesses and diseases. At this time, I entertained one particular thought that would lead me down a path of destruction and depression with a certain amount of insanity. The damage and hurt I inflicted on Linda was incredible.

The thought was, "I wonder why Riana did not contact me for my birthday?" The thought that she had missed my birthday upset me. This thought I had not taken "captive" and given to Christ.

We were going into our eighth week since Linda had rescued me from a dark and deadly future. It had been only four weeks since I fully repented and God delivered me from this evil curse. Linda and I were moving forward in God allowing Him to soothe and heal our marriage. It would have been fine except for that "thought." And, that "thought" is how it all started.

My birthday had come and gone, when I had returned to work. Again, I had this little thought that made me just a little sad. Riana had not wished me a happy birthday. Weird as it seems, this is exactly how the enemy of your soul and of your marriage operates - with little inappropriate ungodly thoughts. How did that thought get into my head?

That morning as I slept, I had a vision of an image come into my mind. I saw a beautiful ornate marriage certificate. It had two names written on it - Riana's and mine. In my vision, I was shocked to see her name on the marriage certificate because I knew I was already married to Linda. But I was not overly concerned about the image. I told Linda about it and she felt I was being overly complacent. At the same time, she questioned her suspicions and felt perhaps, she was overly cautious. How I regret not taking that thought captive and giving it to Jesus.

Understand that spiritual warfare is occurring all the time. There are no breaks from battle, as your enemy is always attempting to outwit you into sin. There can be no complacency in this war. A soldier fights hard and constant. Linda was correct, that I had been overly complacent about the vision.

I walked into my office and there it was - a package from Riana. How did it pass my support group? I should have thrown it away. I should have given it to Maria to destroy. No. I opened it and found that birthday wish I had longed for. Riana sent me a letter and a CD containing some new music. It was the same trap. How could I be so stupid? I was. I had not fully recovered from the magic placed on the previous music she gave me and now I had more! My little thought had flourished into a full-blown action. This action would lead into another action. I was tempted when I was carried away and enticed by my own lust for that gift. Then this lust gave birth to sin, and this sin's ultimate aim was to destroy me (James 1:14, 15).

Well, Riana's birthday was just ten days away. So, I rushed and bought her a gift from an online store and had it delivered. My thinking was that she had been kind enough to send me something, and I should reciprocate. Of course, Linda would not know of this until much later. That day, I called Riana to thank her for the CD she sent me.

Eight weeks into my rescue, and the fourth week to the day since I repented of sin and was delivered by God's grace, I called the very person who had been tormenting Linda and me with spells and curses. I was insane. We talked briefly, and I told her I was staying with my wife, and was calling to thank her for the gift. I was a fool for thinking I was strong enough to talk with her without becoming emotionally involved. I actually deluded myself into thinking I was strong enough to contact her with no affect, and I was actually proud of myself for that as well. I played fast and loose with God's mercy and grace.

I believed that my call was one of courtesy and nothing more. What I failed to realize is that I had opened up that huge demonic portal once again. I had given these demons a legal right to harass me and deceive me. The open door renewed their claim on my soul. Like a fool, I had stepped out from the protection of God. All of the instruction to submit to the authority of Christ and then the protection and healing would occur went in one ear and out the other. This time, the fight would be even more intense.

Evil Transformation

The next day I changed back to my evil self again. My two alter personalities would manifest to Linda when I returned home from work. One personality was very hateful, critical, cynical, irritated, and angry. The other alter personality was dubbed "Paulina" by Linda because it made me cry, whiny, and depressed, like a spoiled little girl. When I walked into our house, I started to become very critical of Linda and had the "I'm disgusted with you" look on my face. Because of the guilt, I began referring to myself as "stupid dog," and a self-loathing oppressive spirit was more than happy to oblige my shame.

Linda could not understand what went wrong. We had made such good progress, so how could these evil spirits descend again on her husband? Of course, I kept secret from Linda the fact that I had received a birthday gift from Riana, I had called her, and I sent her a reciprocal gift. Linda had no idea I had opened up the demonic door again.

As the days rolled by, I was experiencing heavy depression and I struggled to feel alive. I had no joy or peace. Everyday I continued to pray to God and read the Bible because it was the only way I could survive the deep depression. Again, I had been reluctant to attend a "Spirit-filled" church because I had seen so many abuses in church as a young person. I did not like Christians per se, and I certainly did not want any of them to know my business. However, I knew in my heart that I had to have a Spirit-filled man lay his hands on me and pray. So, Linda found a local church that would operate in the gifts of the Spirit.

On the weekend, we went to church but with an intense struggle from the enemy. On arrival, I was already mad as hell and wanted to punch this little imp of an usher in the face for not seating us right away. He made us stand in the back of the church until the pastor gave him the "nod" to seat us. That really got me upset because I waited for no man, and I felt this action was very disrespectful to me, and arrogant of the pastor. I allowed no man to disrespect me. Nevertheless, I finally calmed down and sat. No doubt, Linda was praying. During the service, the Holy Spirit began to draw and convict me. The message was about "fighting for the heart of our King," and I knew I had to make my way to the front, and fall on my face before God. Linda would go with me to make a commitment to fight for the heart of our King.

Amazingly, the church had an altar call. I went up and knelt down, sobbing and praying. Inside I kept repeating to myself, "God, renew my spirit – create in me a clean heart." With my eyes were closed and the worship band blaring out a beautiful song, I felt two hands on me. One hand touched my back while the other touched my heart area. I could not see the face, but heard the voice of a man – a Spirit-filled man.

He prayed aloud repeatedly, "God, renew his spirit and create in him a clean heart." He prayed exactly what I needed. He prayed exactly what was in my heart to pray. The tears flowed from my eyes, and I felt such release. When it was all over, Linda and I searched for the man who had prayed with me, but he was not found. For months, we thought he had been an angel until one night we finally met him. He was a humble beautiful man who was the Spanish Ministry Pastor.

That should have been the end of the second era of demonization, but it was not the end. Why? It was because I still had concealed sin and an open door for the demonic. I still had not confessed to Linda the birthday gift I had received, or the birthday gift I had sent. I also did not confess that I had called Riana a week prior, and in my possession, I had a magical music CD. I was listening to that magical music again. Sure, at church, I prayed and felt a release in my spirit, but I would continually fail to repent and stop sinning. I just wanted the torment to leave, but continue to live as before. This would be a hard lesson for me. God had delivered me a few weeks prior, but now it would take self-discipline to keep that deliverance, self-discipline I lacked.

As I returned to work from the weekend, I would become deeply depressed and sad again. The overwhelming urge to escape reality with Riana would haunt me even though I knew it was not the truth. It was at this time, I fully realized just how deceitful our enemy is. I was a little bird caught in the same old snare over again. Work would be difficult, and this would make me want to escape to a place where I was not frustrated. That place was with Riana, and so my mind continually repeated that sequence. Once again, I could not separate reality from fantasy. I was certainly under the influence of a lying spirit again. The spirit of depression and sadness drove me deeper into despair, not because God's deliverance was not real, rather because I kept dabbling in sin.

One particular night at home, I was so depressed I decided to get drunk and play my guitar loudly through an amplifier. I decided to record the session. As I played, the sadness and despair took over the entire structure of the music. Linda sat beside me amazed at the eerie sounds coming out of my playing. She was hearing me play in a manner she had never heard before. I was creating music I had never played before, and did not know how it was accomplished.

It was as if something else was playing inside of me. After finishing, I labeled the song "sad" and listened to the recording. To my amazement, I had recorded music that I could not reproduce again. The guitar sounds were from hell itself. As a matter of fact, I told Linda the song came from hell. The music I created definitely had a demonic attachment to it. In the future, I would listen to this recording over again as I drove to work, and it always made me sad until the day I destroyed it.

Satan's Social Media

Two days after I had a Spirit-filled man pray over me in church, I returned to work and had a difficult day of depression. I tried to fight it off. This period marked the beginning of the ninth week since my rescue, and Linda and I had made great progress at first, but now I had an open door with concealed sin that was wreaking havoc with me spiritually. So, a difficult day at work magnified my depression and sadness.

Linda had just started her fall semester classes and was away at school on Monday and Wednesday nights. It was not a good thing for me to be alone at night because of the driving urge to connect to Riana. After my repentance and deliverance just five weeks earlier, I was able to be home alone. However, now with my open door to the demonic underworld and concealed sin, I was a sitting duck so to speak. This particular Monday at work had been difficult. The difficulty made me want to escape to a happier time when I had been "vacationing" with Riana. These thoughts then led me to miss that experience and become sad. Inside, I knew it was a pack of lies from Satan, but my mind was so tormented it was difficult to separate the lies from the truth.

As I sat alone at home depressed from the day, and spiritually weak and susceptible from the open demonic door, I received an Email message. The Email was not

110

from Riana because I had been blocking all of her messages. Her tactic was to send me packages via mail to my office using different return addresses so not to arouse my suspicions. No, this Email came from Riana's friend, the vampire witch. The subject line read, "The quintessential road trip." The body of the Email only contained a hyperlink to an outside webpage. The Email got through because only Riana's Email address had been blocked, not her friend's Email address. She had never sent me anything before, so it was strange to hear from her.

I should have shivered in disgust and deleted it, I should have had the sense to curb my curiosity, I should have known better by now. But, I did not. I found myself "clicking" on the hyperlink. Alone, depressed, weak, and curious, I made a horrible mistake and I felt it physically hook me just as a fishhook would capture its prey. I was so stupid.

The hyperlink took me to a social media website created by Riana. As the website opened, "our song," the one that came to me in a dream and the one that haunted me in the dentist's chair, began to play. The website was dark with a video clip of burning candles. Below the candles was a picture of Riana beckoning me to explore further. It was the weirdest feeling. I felt a physical twist or hook inside my chest as soon as the song began to play. I stood over the computer screen and literally laughed because I knew she got me. I understood I had fallen for a trap and became captive once again. I really was a stupid dog.

Like a moth drawn to its destruction in a flame, I began to read her website. Everything I had blocked out from her emails was now in front of me to read. Music, stories, and pictures used to lure me in like an animal into a cage. I read stories I felt directly aimed at me. I felt she was communicating messages to me because she knew I would eventually end up looking at her social media website. I was hooked. I was again mesmerized. I read everything on her website for the next few days.

Within a day, I brought trouble on both Linda and me. While asleep, Linda heard a voice telling her to check the time. She awoke and looked at the clock. It read the familiar 2:05 AM. Linda then heard a voice in her head mocking her and telling her to pray. She started to pray over me because I was restless although I could not remember any dreams or visions. That morning, I had a very different attitude than before. I refused to pray to God or read His Word. The spiritual warfare book I was reading, I put aside because it was irritating me.

I told Linda that there are things that we have no control over and one of them is the battle that is going on inside my head, and so I was not going to fight it any longer, rather, just let it be. The reader can see the strategy of our enemy attempting to convince me not to fight for my thoughts. If I opened the gate, refusing to shut it, then the enemy would have all the access he needed until total demolition was accomplished. Linda continued to pray for me, seeking God's guidance and wisdom. At this point, she believed my depressed

112

attitude was the result of my work at the police department. Again, she was not aware of my hidden sins.

Then, Wednesday rolled around. Linda had a night class, and I was left alone with my computer and sin. After work, I fixed my favorite whiskey, and proceeded to get drunk. With that, I had built once again my danger house, which consisted of high emotion, aloneness, and mind-altering drugs (alcohol). I opened up that dangerous social media website and began to examine fervently everything going on in Riana's life. It was a method of being involved with her without having to read her Emails or letters. She would never know I was studying her life, Linda would never know, and so that made it all right, I thought.

However, this time was different. I perceived some negative comments that she had written about me. I read one story about a "stupid dog" and a controlling woman over the dog. I believed Riana was attacking Linda and me in her short story. Then other messages and images appeared spitefully directed toward me, and I became very angry and hurt at the same time. Because of my drunken condition, my emotions raged, and I called her.

I turned into "Paulina" and began to cry, expressing my hurt over her comments about me. The next day, on her birthday she telephoned, and was concerned about my safety. She told me that she had checked many local news outlets to see if I had killed myself. That is how bad I cried the night before. And that would be the last time I would ever speak to her.

When Linda returned from night class, she found me drunk playing my guitar again. I told her "no more religious stuff" because I was disappointed I had not received my "miracle" from God. I also wanted her to tell my family to quit talking the religious stuff to me. My disappointment with God was now turning into anger.

Preparing for the Worst

Nine weeks to the very day since Linda rescued me from Riana, I confessed to Linda my sin in contacting Riana. I was deeply sorrowful and returned emotionally to where I had first started. I felt I had failed Linda, and wasted all of our valuable progress we had made up to this point in time. I was a "cheater" and could not stop myself. I had contacted Riana just as she predicted I would. I was one sorry soul.

As our support group was briefed about my recent actions, they advised Linda to leave me. My family gave her permission to leave me. There was no sympathy for my behavior anymore. Even Linda felt this was enough. She asked the Lord for wisdom and then, she gave me the ultimatum. I had to choose. It was either Linda or Riana, but I could not have both. Linda made it clear that my decision would be final. If I stayed with Linda, I was to break all contact with Riana for good. If I chose to be with Riana, I would not ever be able to reconcile with Linda.

114

Linda took a hard stand with me, but she had to in order to preserve her sanity and wellbeing. She would not condone this behavior. It was no longer just Satan tormenting me through a love spell, but my own inability to exercise self-control and discipline. Linda and our support group were correct. I was being a self-centered, disrespectful husband.

Although she did not want to, Linda had to start preparing for the worse. I was going to leave her for another woman. I had lied to her and betrayed her. My secret sin would be the breaking point of any frail trust we might have had. Linda felt in her heart that I was already gone, and now she had to pick up the pieces and move forward. All of her support group was telling her the same thing, leave him. Even our marriage counselor gave Linda permission to let me go. This was it. This was the end.

My personality would shift back and forth between the sobbing, pathetic little girl we called, "Paulina" and my real character. In our conversations, one moment I would miss my freedom and happiness I had experienced, and then the next I would be telling Linda how much I loved her and did not want to lose her. I was mental. I felt insane. I agreed at this time to seek some professional assistance from a counselor through my employment. Because I thought all of my issues stemmed from work-related stress, I believed seeking counseling in this area was the best course of action.

I did not really want to leave my wife, but I simply could not resist the urge to return to this witch any longer. I told Linda to "protect herself" financially, and I would understand what she had to do. It appeared that Riana had won. The only thing preventing me from going down to ruin was Linda. Because I had hurt her so badly, I had run the risk of losing her also. Once Linda was out of the way, there could be nothing to stop Riana from having me. But, then there was God, and losing me was not in His plans. I belonged to Him and not to myself.

Chapter 7: The Second Chance

The Voice

It was a Friday evening and we were to attend the musical play *Grease*. First Linda and I drove to my mother's house for prayer. I needed to repent of my secret sins and make things right with God. Leaving my mother's house, we arrived at the play, and I told Linda that I had not "felt" anything during the prayer session. My mood was beginning to sour. Suddenly, the oppressive, angry spirit was upon me. Linda started to pray to God. She felt fear, but fought it with prayer. She was pushing hard to trust God, as she knew I was under demonic influence again.

This happened to be a nice warm night at an outdoor play with me being in an exceptionally foul mood. I hated the world. Being cranky, miserable, sad and confused, I arrived and looked at everyone around me having a good time. I just could not understand how they could be so happy. Their happiness annoyed me greatly. I stared at them with disgust and hate. Linda saw some people she knew, she waved and briefly talked with them. I knew them also through a mutual friend, but I just looked at them with hate. They were smiling. I could not understand why.

As the play started, I felt like a ship tossed in the ocean. My mind was extremely unstable. One moment I wanted to leave my marriage, the next moment I wanted to make it work. I was on a dime's edge, creating an

117

exit strategy from my marriage, and then suddenly running to the other edge to create a stability strategy for my marriage. I felt like I was losing my mind. So, what happened next could be chocked-off as mental illness, a mental breakdown of sorts, but why did it transform me? I caution the reader. This gets very strange, but it happened to me. All I know is this very strange occurrence happened and changed me from an unstable victim to decisive combatant.

While the play was going on, about 9:00 PM, I heard a voice in my head. It was not an audible voice rather, one so loud in my head that I actually had a conversation with it. I had a real give-and-take dialogue with this voice. I tried to play tricks with the voice and make it say things I wanted it to say, but it would correct me, tell me it had a short amount of time with me, command me to listen to it, and then proceed to give me guidance and instruction. I went into a trance, literally. I had a conversation with this voice for the entire second act of the play. Yes, for about an hour, I was in a trance-like state having a discussion with a voice inside my head. When I awoke, the band on stage was playing their last musical number, and I was a different man. I have no recollection of anything else but of this particular conversation.

Voice: "Listen, I don't have much time so you need to listen to me. Your wife, Linda, is a good woman. Look at her. She is beautiful, smart, and loving. Do not throw your marriage away for another woman."

I was shocked at the intrusion of this voice in the middle of a play, and so I tried to toy with it and make it say things. I tested it by attempting to make it say positive things about the other woman like, "She is real nice. I like her." But, the voice firmly rebuked me.

Voice: "Paul, listen to me! Paul, listen to me!"

I could not make the voice go to the other side in the conversation, so I decided to listen to it. As I listened, I wondered if I was really going insane. Had I actually lost my mind? Could there really be a message for me in the voice?

Voice: "Paul, you can't leave Linda."

I replied, "You don't know this other woman. She needs me. She is sad without me, and waiting for my return. I stomped on her heart before, and now I will do it again if I do not go to her. I can't hurt her anymore."

Voice: "You are right, I don't know this other woman, but I do know Linda. The one thing I do know is Linda, and she is a good, beautiful woman that needs your love, attention, and focus. You feel bad for hurting this other woman, and you should feel bad. What you have done is wrong, and caused many people pain. However, you cannot save her. You want to save her from her pain, and you are willing to throw away your loving marriage to save someone you can't possibly save."

Then the voice reminded me of other people in my past that I felt compelled to save, to rescue, and to help. I was reminded of specific situations, which I became emotionally involved in, not because of love rather,

119

because of my "knight in shining armor" complex. I realized long ago that every time I did this, I ended up trapped and pulled down – like swimming into quicksand to save someone. I had never been able to save anyone. The relationships ended broken and painful. The voice assured me that my relationship with Riana would be no different. Now, the voice said something stunning to me. Something I never heard before, or ever thought prior.

Voice: "Look at your marriage to Linda. You did not marry her because she needed saving. Saving Linda was not necessary. You did not marry Linda to save her, but she is married to you to save you! You cannot leave her. She is the only person that can help you in this time of crisis. This is her job with you – to save you! You need to pay attention to Linda in little ways. She needs you Paul. You need to find the little meaningful things and respond in love to Linda."

The voice changed directions and began to discuss the other woman. It warned me not to hate her because the hate would return to me. It revealed the fact that Riana was mentally unstable, and magnifies my kind gestures a hundred times, accelerating her feelings of love for me in an unrealistic manner.

Voice: "When you give her a gift, some conversation, some attention, she takes this to mean you love her when you only meant it to be kind. You cannot do this! She will get hurt, as she has been hurt in the past due to her clinginess to men. Her clinginess to you will drive you insane in a very short while. You cannot save her

120

from this. She has abnormal, unrealistic, and accelerated expectations of true love from a married man. Paul, you must stay away from her!"

How could this voice possibly know so much about Riana? These were thoughts that I had never imagined. Since placed under a delusional love spell, I always defended Riana. These observations from the voice were shocking, but rang true. Yet, there was more to be heard.

Voice: "Paul, listen. Your mind is troubled and divided, and you are having all sorts of problems with depression and instability. The religious things you are doing such as, attending church, meditating on Scripture, praying to God, receiving prayer, and begging for a miracle are beneficial and good. But, these things cannot help you if your mind is split in two.

"Paul, the answer you seek is simple. It is not hard. Simply make a commitment and quit dividing your mind. Stay with your wife and shun the other woman. Commit to your marriage and to loving Linda and the rest will take care of itself. Then, and only then, will the religious acts you perform have an impact. You have to decide what you want to do – go with someone you can't possibly save and drown yourself, or stay with the one who is saving you."

As the voice stopped speaking to me, I became conscious of the play's ending musical number. It was so weird I started to cry with joy. The answers to my questions were now clear. I had direction and instruction. I had my miracle. My mood transformed from hate and despondency to love and elation. I was stunned with the release I felt. I looked over at Linda intently watching the play, unaware of what had just happened to me. I felt so much love for her.

As soon as the music stopped, I excitedly told Linda what had happened. Although believing me, she was shocked. Yet, she noticed that I looked very peaceful. She said that I had held her hand during the second half of the show, and so she knew that the oppressive spirit had left me. It was obvious I was a different man than the one whom she walked in with earlier. We talked about it on the way home, and Linda encouraged me to write everything down. At 10:00 PM that night, I sat down and documented the occurrence in an Email to all of my praying family. I did not care if anyone believed me or not. The voice talked to me and gave me the instruction and guidance I desperately needed.

The next morning, one of my sisters told Linda and me that she had been praying for us the night before at about 9:00 PM. This was the exact time that I heard the voice in my head. While praying at this time, she had asked God to speak to me because she knew I would not listen to anyone else. We can only give God the glory.

God Takes Control

The next morning after having the conversation with the "voice," I woke up, looked at Linda, and said, "I'm back!" God had delivered me once again, and now I was going to do my part to stay clean and sober. That

Saturday evening we went back to the Pentecostal church. The message was clear. It was about submitting to Christ. God is in control. Linda and I responded to the altar call once again, and I wept like a baby. I fell on my face before God, repenting of and confessing my sins. God touched me and I felt God move upon me that night. Again, I had a Spirit-filled man lay hands on me and pray over my heart, soul, and mind. A big broken man had fallen prostrate before his Creator, sobbing uncontrollably for forgiveness and for assistance. This time I knew I needed more than only relief from my demonic tormentors, I needed a renewed spirit inside of me. I needed to grow in a relationship with God. I must become a new creature.

Immediately, I started hearing the voice of God inside. He told me to get "His Word into my soul." I had to start saturating myself in Scripture. This was imperative. I also had to take up the full armor of God so that I could resist in the evil day (Ephesians 6:13). Yet, I was worried. I had fallen before, and I was overly concerned that I would fall again. I had to learn to really trust in God for His sustaining power.

While this was going on with me, Linda had decided to submit to God rather than to me. If I were to go sideways again, she would not follow me down the path of destruction. She had to place God first in her life, not me. She said, "Paul, I am going to follow Christ no matter what you do. You can follow Christ with me or go in another direction, but for me, I am committing to God with all of my heart." Linda's revelation also assisted me at work because now I could submit to God first, and then submit to the men He placed as bosses over me. I could work as for God unless I was required to do something unethical or against God's law.

Of course, the demonic attacks would not subside. But, not because of an open door and invitation rather because this is how we were to learn and grow in recognizing our enemy. This is how we would be trained to take up the authority of our Lord Jesus Christ against an already defeated enemy.

And of course just the natural feelings stemming from such a trauma also plagued us, but especially Linda was affected. My second fall had really devastated her. She naturally had "trust issues" with me. She had been so strong for my first fall because I was like a deceived victim of witchcraft (although I was not innocent in my behavior by any stretch of the imagination). But since my "re-contact" and subsequent demonization, I had put Linda through the emotional paces.

My roller coaster emotions coupled with my extreme insensitivity and denial had left her raw and exposed. Only God could heal our marriage. Nothing I could do at this point could re-knit us. It would take another miracle from God for Linda to totally forgive me and for me to totally depend on Him in cementing our love. Linda could not trust me, but she could trust God.

Feelings vs. Knowledge

Going into the tenth week since Linda rescued me, I was having a hard time with everything. God was teaching me "it is not what you feel – it is what you know." It is what you know! What did I know? God's Word is truth is all I knew. That is why the Lord instructed me to saturate myself in His Word. I would need to hang onto every bit of truth, learning not to rely on my feelings as an indicator of my spiritual status.

I would wake up in the morning "feeling" blah. Because I did not "feel" joy or elation, I assumed something was wrong in my commitment to God. It was not. Feelings come and go but God's Word is truth, and that is what I needed to hang onto. Four days after repenting at church and being instructed to get Scripture into me, I tried. While driving to work, I eagerly awaited listening to various radio ministers coming on the airwaves during my commute. But, my smart phone device constantly interrupted me with Emails, phone calls, and text messages. Because I had to lead a large police bureau, these interruptions could not be ignored causing me to miss the entire messages of God's Word. It was very frustrating.

Arriving at work, I noticed an Email from Riana was waiting for me. I had unblocked her communications to me during my second fall and failed to re-block her Emails. I read it, deleted it, and emptied the digital trash, believing that was adequate. My support group at work was gone, and I was alone. I was feeling bad. I kept repeating, "His grace is sufficient. If only just for today, His grace is sufficient."

So, I held onto my resurrection through the death and resurrection of Christ. My feelings did not want to be crucified with Christ. I wanted a coffee latte forgetting all of this hard fought spiritual battle stuff. It was hard strenuous work. However, I knew that it would pass.

I knew (because of the Word) that someday I would find and enter into God's rest. It was not a feeling. It was knowledge. Perhaps not that day or the next, but I knew it would happen because God's Word said it would. I reminded myself I was a bondservant to Christ. My mother had dedicated me as a small child to God, and she meant it. It was not just a Sunday morning ritual for her. That is where it all started. I was presented to God as a living sacrifice. I belonged to Him. That is what I "knew."

Closing the Doors

The next day at work, I received more Emails from Riana. Instead of deleting them forthright, I read them first and then deleted them. Again, thinking this was adequate. I did not respond to her, but I still read the Emails, and that was wrong behavior. This behavior needed to be submitted to Christ. It was leaving an open door for demons to have legal access to my life. Yes, God had delivered me, but I now needed to exercise discipline over my "flesh."

Of course that night I became depressed. My mood began to change into "Paulina." Linda found me discouraged, frustrated, cynical, doubting, angry with God, and rejecting her advice. Before we went to bed, Linda prayed and asked God to show me what I was doing wrong.

At midnight, I woke up to the smell of fresh brewed coffee. I remembered the words in my head from the last time I smelled this coffee. "Wake up and smell the coffee." It was Riana beckoning me again. I suddenly felt this dark evil presence surround me. I could hear thumping noises in our room. Then at about 3:45 AM, Linda woke up and had the desire to pray over me. She heard God tell her to pray on my behalf. She felt the evil in our room just hovering over me.

Then the Lord opened Linda's heart. He revealed that the doors to the demonic were kept open through the Emails from Riana that I was opening and reading. As long as I continued to open and read those spell-infused Emails, I would give Satan and his demons a legal right to torment me, eventually destroying me.

I woke up with Linda telling me what the Lord had revealed to her. I laughed because while asleep, He told me the same thing. I needed to repent and stop. The next morning, the oppressive "Paulina" spirit had left me, and I was back to being myself. I knew what I had to do. Now it seems so obvious, but at the time, I was so pig headed, and ignorant of the enemy's tactics. I was a slow learner.

Linda reminded me it had been a long time since I had exercised my spiritual muscles. Always doing things my way, now having to submit to the authority of Christ, was hard for me. I had to learn obedience. In order to win this battle for my mind, body, and soul, I had to "stand" in obedience. While I was learning obedience, Linda learned to trust in God to fulfill His Word in our lives.

By the end of the week, I had my first counseling session with a professional service. To my surprise, the counselor was a Christian woman. I told her my story of anger, adultery, demonization, along with my current struggles to remain clean and sober. She agreed that I needed help! Because she was a Christian, she understood my issues on a spiritual level also. This was a real blessing for me. I also told her about my extreme anger directed at my bosses at work, and about my work frustrations. It looked like I was moving in a positive direction. However, I still had to close every door and every opportunity for the enemy of my marriage to harass me.

Spirits Still Hover

This heavy spirit would still come upon me at any given time, and we had to be careful what I exposed myself to. For example, one night we were going out to the movies, and Linda could see I was uncomfortable going inside because there were too many people around. We were careful and left for another smaller historic theater. Yet, as I entered into the theater I started feeling ill. It was like a pressure inside my chest and I wanted to cry for no reason at all. Linda could sense this oppressive spirit "Paulina" hovering over me just waiting for any opportunity to influence.

The "Paulina" spirit had apparently been trying to get to me all day, as Linda had noticed earlier in the day when

I was outside watering some plants I had that trance-like stare in my eyes. She knocked on the window to get my attention. I smiled, but she could see that I was simply not there. Unbeknownst to me, Linda had gone into her prayer room and prayed to God on my behalf. When I returned inside, I was normal again.

Now in the theater, Linda would do the same. She would pray over me, saying the name of Jesus repeatedly, reciting Scripture in her mind over again. The Lord whispered to her, "Trust me." Linda told God, "I will trust You, Lord," and she felt a peace. She looked over at me, and saw that I was present mentally and engaged in the movie.

Then I started to feel demonic heat again. It was a common occurrence for both Linda and I when "they" were around. Linda touched me and could feel my clammy skin. My internal body became hotter and hotter. I prayed, covering myself in the blood of Jesus, and quoting Scripture. The heat left me. But, before the spirit leaving, I felt Riana was conducting some sort of incantation to try to reach me. Linda was sensing it too.

At home, I was better, but still not completely free. I would tell Linda how messed up I was, and as we slept I would hold her close because touching her made me feel safe and secure.

Linda would continue to awake in the middle of the night, and pray over me. Then falling asleep, she would have dreams of me leaving her. She had to continually rebuke the thoughts and quote the Scripture; "We are taking every thought captive to the obedience of Christ," (2Corinthians 10:5).

Spiritual warfare is exactly that, warfare. It is a constant, unrelenting battle of the mind. God does not fight it for you, He expects you to fight this battle in His authority and power. You have the tools and authority through Christ Jesus. Every Biblical Christian needs to learn this truth in order to free themselves from the bondage of the flesh and demonic influence, which keeps the believer from being completely effective in the Kingdom of God.

Accountability to God

As I would pray to God, He would speak to my heart. I would get insights that I knew had not come from inside me. He reminded me of the day Linda came and rescued me from Riana the witch. He said, "Paul, that day when you cut your ties with Riana you did it for Linda. And the day Doug destroyed every idol in your office from Riana you did it for him. Paul, now you must never contact her again, and this time you do it for Me." It was God telling me to be obedient to Him.

He did not want my sacrifice. He wanted my obedience. Going to church, praying, reading Scripture was fine, but He wanted my obedience. I was continually breeching the angelic protection surrounding me, and giving the enemy power when I would yield to thoughts about Riana. My mind could no longer be divided. This was very serious. If I were to re-contact Riana, God would hold me accountable and deal with me. I was no longer a "victim" of a witch's spell, but a believer accountable to the Lord Jesus Christ.

Linda was free to love me, and trust God to deal with my behaviors. She realized that I was no longer accountable to our marriage, but directly accountable to God. Another violation of trust would not be targeted to Linda only, but a sin directly violating God's command to me. This fact freed Linda from having to be suspicious and untrusting of me. I was now accountable to a higher source, a much higher source.

It had been revealed to me that had I not re-contacted Riana, our torment would be over. I learned a valuable lesson. It was a big teachable moment for me, and the respect of the consequences of disobedience had been firmly planted in my mind. I started to have real good days without demonic thoughts, depression, and oppressive spirits hovering over me. I had a dream of a large rattlesnake outside of our bedroom patio door peering in. Linda and I knew that it was a warning dream to stay alert.

Linda was praying to God "for a normal life again" when she stopped and changed her prayer to "not my will Lord, but Your will be done." Our marriage would never be the same again. It would consist of a new "normal" that was far from the average couple's normal. Linda would continually quote, "I have been crucified with Christ; and it is no longer I who live, but Christ lives in me; the life I now live in the flesh, I live by faith in the Son of God, who loved me and gave Himself up for me," (Galatians 2:20). Interestingly, this was a Scripture Linda had heard a year before my adultery, and it grabbed her attention. She committed it to memory and recited it every day for a month. This Scripture was her strong confidence during my entire rescue.

In 1Corinthians 13, it says that "love bears all things, believes all things, hopes all things, endures all things, and love never fails." Linda would hold onto this Scripture and pray to God to create true love in our marriage. She committed this truth to memory, and prayed that God would manifest it in her heart. She wanted to love me with a sincere heart and with God's unconditional love.

Going into the eleventh week since my rescue, Linda woke up at 3:45 AM and was impressed to pray over me, which she did. She prayed for God's protection and guidance. She also requested the Lord assist me with obedience to him, and to fill my mind and heart with truth. The next morning, I actually looked refreshed. I had not been refreshed in a long time. The obedience to God's command was very beneficial. When I left for work that morning, I told Linda, "I am going to have a good day." The Lord had revealed to me that He was sending angelic re-enforcements ahead, and all I had to do was "obey." Linda knew then that there was something bad waiting for me at work, and I was going to be tested in obedience. She was not anxious or worried rather felt peace and assurance that it was going to be fine. I told Linda I would send her a "praise report" later in the day.

Demons Don't Give Up

When I arrived at my office, my desk was piled high as usual with mail and paperwork. I saw a "Federal Express" package sent certified requiring a signature for acceptance. The staff working at the front lobby of the police station had signed for the package and then delivered it to my office. The return address was from the city where Riana resided, but this was not unusual because I had many projects waiting in that city. And so I opened the package.

Once opened, I saw another package inside sealed with tape with Riana's return address on it. There was no question this was another demonic influenced package from a woman not giving up easily. Emails, telephone calls, and letters in the mail were not working on me anymore, and so another way to get me to open up her spell bound writings was to send them certified mail. However, this time I had no desire to open it, allowing the open door into the spiritual abyss. I immediately called Doug, gave him the package, which he promptly destroyed.

I telephoned Linda to tell her of the "praise report," and we both rejoiced in God. I had passed this test in obedience. I was beginning to realize the Spirit of God would not wrestle with someone who continually disobeys His commands. That person would become a reprobate, and I certainly did not want that. Trust and obedience were essential.

Just two days after receiving the certified mail package, she sent another one. It was the same scenario, a staff worker at the police station signed for it and placed it on my desk. Now, Riana was getting very desperate. I had no support group around me that day, so I destroyed the package myself. It was weird, and now I felt like she was stalking me.

It was not just about me. Linda was having all kinds of strange thoughts about me not loving her. Naturally, she would be insecure after my infidelity, but her thoughts would take her to deep dark depressing places. If I did not return a text message, she felt rejected. If I was not totally engaged in our conversation, she took that as a sign I did not love her. Whereas, at first she was strong, she was now becoming weak and insecure. This was another tactic of the enemy to try to separate us from each other.

However, considering the circumstances that Linda was under, it was a difficult situation for her because it was only normal to feel rejection and insecurities. Yet, the enemy would take advantage and magnify those feelings with distorted imaginations making her feel inconsequential. We knew we had to move forward together, not separately.

As we were heading into the twelfth week since my rescue, we realized so much had happened in that horrible three-month time span. It was the absolute worst three-month period of our lives. God had told me to get his Word into me at all costs. I was saturating myself with Christian radio, television, DVDs, church, Bible, and everything I could get my hands on with God's Word contained in it. It was literally giving me life and strength, needed to go through those terrible months.

Linda was attending night classes on Wednesdays, and so I needed to find a Bible study somewhere. I remember the first night I tried to attend. First, my boss kept me at work later than normal, so late I had to rush to get to church. As I neared the church, I became disoriented and lost. I could not find it. As I drove in panic, I could hear Satan say, "See, I won." But, I told Satan, "Even if I have to arrive there when it is over and simply touch the door, then you have not won. You will have to kill me to prevent me from getting to church!"

I continued to drive aimlessly. Finally, I found the church and arrived during the very last ten minutes of the sermon. The ushers would not allow me inside, because "it would disturb others." So, I sat in the lobby with all the mothers and their screaming babies, with all the teenagers who did not want to be there, with all the ushers and greeters wanting to converse with one another. Yet, I heard the last ten minutes of God's Word, and Satan lost! He could not kill me, and I had arrived. So, I felt strengthened in my obedience. I would continue to attend every Wednesday night with Linda joining me later after she finished class.

The evil spirits were relentless in trying to confuse and separate Linda and me. It was a real spiritual battle, and we were being trained up as warriors. We just did not know it at the time. The demons attacked us mostly through depression and discouragement. It was Monday morning, and I was fully depressed and discouraged on my way to work. Linda could see it all over my face. She recognized the spirit over me as "Paulina," which expresses itself as depressed and sad. I felt like I was losing my mind on this roller coaster spiritual battle. One day I was depressed, the next day I was fine in God, and then the next day depressed again. It was exhausting for the both of us. I could not seem to gain complete victory in my life.

As I left for work, I had my second appointment in the afternoon with a professional counselor. I was not looking forward to it. Linda prayed over me. God gave her Ephesians 6:12, which states that we do not fight against flesh and blood rather against spiritual forces of darkness and wickedness in the air. God was reminding Linda that the things "seen" are temporal while the working of God is "eternal."

The Diagnosis

I went to my counseling session with a Christian counselor. I told her our story, and I could see her shock at what I was saying. She confirmed that I was extremely depressed, and under too much stress in too many areas. The affair caused stress, working on my marriage caused stress, work caused stress, and even my "faith" caused stress. She gave me specific recommendations. First, I had to limit my alcohol consumption to four drinks per week; second, set my alarm earlier to get out of the house sooner; and third, get a medical exam to rule out any physical causes for my depression. Our first marriage therapist diagnosed me as having posttraumatic stress disorder. Now, this therapist was essentially saying the same thing. I was one messed up guy.

The next day, as I drove to work I tried to listen to Christian radio, but the teachers were debating stupid things instead of proclaiming God's Word. What a waste of airtime. I could not stand it any longer, so I put in a teaching CD, but I had heard it many times before and so I was bored with it. I then decided to put in my old rock music that had spell casting on it. I listened to that evil-infused music all the way to work, and it made me sadder still and even more depressed. But, it was like wiggling a loose tooth, and it felt good in a weird way. However, I Emailed Linda and confessed to her my disobedience. It was a disgusting thing to hear preachers and teachers discuss politics and science with every other topic in this fallen world, but fail to declare God's truth to people who are in dire need of it. I was at my wits end with all this demon stuff. Why could I not hold onto my deliverance?

Chapter 8: The Tap Out

Submission

Just one day before my twelve-week rescue anniversary, I was fed-up with Christian radio, pastoral teaching CDs, and the entire demonic attack scenario. Perhaps, I was just crazy as a bat. Then it happened. The life-changing event that would give me the sustained victory I desperately needed. First, allow me to explain a little background.

When I was training in the martial arts, I used to practice Brazilian style Ju-Jitsu with some very good martial artists. They would always win. No matter how hard I tried to beat them, they would calmly place me in a position where I had to "tap out," or surrender to them. Because they were so good, they would never hurt me, just put enough uncomfortable pressure on one of my joints or limbs to make me submit.

What happened to me spiritually with God was no different. I went to sleep that night after listening for hours to my demonic-infused rock music. This music was very powerful, and always made me sad and depressed. It was my Kryptonite so to speak. I knew I should not have done so, but the irritating preachers on the radio forced me to sin, so I thought. As I went to sleep totally disgusted and despondent, sometime in the night, a Word from the Lord came to me. What I heard was, "Paul, you have to tap out. You have to submit to God."

When I woke up in the morning, I knew what I had to do! It seems so simple now, but back then I was full of pride and anger. Although, I went through the motions of obeying God, and I desperately wanted His help, I failed to "surrender" my life to Him as the superior being. Now I knew I had to surrender all to Him. No more lip service, no more pretending, no more whining, no more feeling victimized, and no more willful disobedience and sinning! Moreover, that little bit of knowledge turned everything around for me.

The first thing upon waking, I said to Linda, "I need to submit to God!" I jumped out of bed, and began praying earnestly to God. I gave up to him. I surrendered all. All to Jesus my precious Savior, I surrendered all. I meant it. I finally just "taped out" and submitted. My whole countenance changed. The depression left. My mind became clearer. It was different from that time forward, and it has never been the same again. I was removed from the deep pit I was in, and now I was in the light of God's wonderful grace. I saw a vision of me in a deep dark pit, eating maggots, but I thought it was steak. Once my eyes were opened to the truth, I realized the disgusting lifestyle I had led.

On my way to work, I was different. My attitude changed. I no longer needed to listen to that spell bound music, and I could enjoy the Word of God. I could tell there had been a marked change inside of me. The heavy burden of demonic oppression was gone. This was a definitive demarcation line in my life. Submitting my life to God made all the difference in whether I would be victorious in spiritual battle or a common casualty.

I arrived at work, and found yet another package on my desk. This time sent priority mail. Satan would be relentless in trying to overcome Linda and me. I threw the package away into the shredder. No way was I going back to that dark pit of sadness and depression. Therefore, on the anniversary of the twelfth week since my rescue, I was a new man. It felt good to be in Christ. The entire world seemed different from before, and my priorities began to change.

I went into a business meeting with my boss, whom I particularly disliked. As I watched him work and communicate in this meeting, suddenly I felt a respect for him. This was huge for me because in the past, I respected no man. This change in heart started a new and fruitful relationship. I was shocked that I actually found another man I could admire. Jesus was changing me fast. The fact is some things in our carnal nature come off quickly and effortlessly, and other things take a long time to be removed.

The Holy Spirit does His work on a person, and in His time, the human elements that hinder us are shaved and shattered. We are justified before God after Jesus removes our sins, and then we go through the sanctification process to become blameless before him. It can take years before the Holy Spirit reveals to a person some of their strongholds and thought patterns that prevent them from walking in complete fullness with God. One of my big strongholds was anger.

I was not angry all the time. Nevertheless, when it came up, it came up hard, and the possibility of me doing something stupid was increased. Honestly, it took years to finally defeat this evil part of my nature and only after the Holy Spirit imparted some hard revelation to me. I always thought I would get angry with people because I spent twenty-five plus years as a police officer and had seen the armpit of society for too long. Possibly this is a decent reason, but not an entirely good justification. I reasoned, "It's just the way I am." However, it took several years before I accepted the fact that it was a demonic thought, a demonic lie, and a demonic action that caused my hate for some people.

Instead of being under the influence of a demon, something I could not control, my anger was a "hot button" to get me to sin. Satan knows what "buttons to push." If one's weakness is lust, you can bet a sexy dressed woman is going to cross your path. If the weakness is fear, Satan will place something before you to make you afraid and distrusting of God. All he needs is an open door; just a little crack in your armor will suffice.

If you are enticed and drawn away by your own lust, and give into it, it will produce sin, and of course, when sin is completed it produces death (James 1:14, 15). My hot buttons were people. Almost anything they did could set me off; standing too close to me, the look on someone's face, their children, the way they drove, pushing their shopping cart in the middle aisle, or just about any other benign behavior that I perceived as irritating. However, mostly baseless reasons would attract my ire. Yet, over time, God would reveal and convict me of these things, sanctifying me for his purpose.

God's Remedies

The weekend came, and Linda and I went to church on Saturday night. It was wonderful just being bathed in God's Word and worship. Yet, Satan was not giving up the fight easily. He would attempt many methods to open up a door for demonic influence. Both Linda and I had to be fully alert and aware continually. We were in the heat of battle, and the enemy was launching new attacks every moment. He coordinated his attacks through dreams, songs, and inappropriate thoughts.

Early Sunday morning about 1:00 A.M., I woke up with this particular rock song in my head. The song was a sad one about a relationship gone badly. I had purchased this music myself but while under the influence of a demonic spell. This music had the exact same affect on me as the music Riana had given to me. The song was audible to my ears just as if it was coming from a radio. It was so clear it woke me up. I lied in bed with this tune in my brain, and I was afraid that it would soon make me sad. I knew that trying to fight it off with pure mental will power was futile. It was like telling someone not to think about the large pink elephant in the room. The first thing they are going to do is to think about that elephant. Then I purposely tried to replace the rock song with a worship song. The words, melody, and even the chord progression of a beautiful worship song began to flood my mind, and erase the rock tune. This was God's remedy. He had given me an original worship song.

I got out of bed to write the song down, and when I returned to bed, I looked at the clock, which read "2:05 AM." Normally this satanic time of the morning would have frightened me, but not this time. I laughed, prayed, and thanked God for the wonderful song. I fell asleep in peace. Again, this was God's remedy.

That morning I was sick with a cold. Linda and I stayed home on a Sunday and talked. We both felt that Riana and her witch friend were attempting to spell cast again. We could both sense a "drawing in" similar to a spiritual gravitational pull. The thought came to me that I should contact Riana and tell her that our relationship was completely dissolved, and to move on and leave me alone. The thought came as a "leadership" thought. As a leader, I owed it to this person to politely explain things just as I would have explained it to any other subordinate officer. The enemy is very subtle in his ability to plant an inappropriate thought. I prayed about this idea, and the Lord gave me a definite "No!" God said to me once again, "Do not ever contact Riana again. Any contact no matter how sincere would be misunderstood and give her false hope. Contact was extremely dangerous, and forbidden." I thanked God for his remedy.

That Sunday night as I fell asleep, Linda and I had strange and frightful dreams. I saw visions of occult pentagrams and symbols. I saw occult rituals. Then in my dream vision, I saw Riana's witch friend with many other people marching around in a graveyard chanting unrecognizable words. This vision was very disturbing. Linda had dreams of Riana and tormenting dreams of the past. We firmly believe these witches were actually performing more spell casting rituals on us. Linda had a strong sense that these two witches were extremely angry with her, and wanted her out of the way so that Riana could get to me. The plan was to have Linda commit suicide

The next day on Monday, I returned to work a changed man. I had my third counseling session in the afternoon, and I struggled hard to find anything wrong with me! God had removed all of those oppressive spirits, and I was seeing much more clearly now. I arrived at my session, sat down, and began to articulate to the counselor what had happened since I submitted to Christ's authority over me. I had no issues! I even told her how I saw value in my boss, and actually respected his intellect. She told me that what God had taught me was absolutely "text book," and there could be no other help coming from a human being. That was the last time I attended a therapy session. God had healed me, and He would heal my marriage.

Chapter 9: The New Target

The Warnings

Because Linda experienced something unique in the area of outside curses on her life, she will take over our story from this point. I (Linda) woke up that Monday morning feeling an invisible ball on my forehead. I was highly depressed and weepy for no reason, and wanted to die. The feeling was very strong. I prayed and gave it to the Lord. I also claimed the blood of Christ continually confessing my standing in Him. In all this, still I could sense the anger of Riana and her witch friend toward me.

That night, while asleep, Paul heard a voice telling him to wake-up. When he opened his eyes, he saw the clock, and again it read, 2:05 AM. He looked over at me as I slept, and because all seemed fine he went back to sleep. He would later learn to engage in prayer over his family when things like this occurred.

I was about to get attacked full force by a demonic curse placed on me from Riana and her witch friend. Both Paul and I noticed that strange things began to happen to me during the time of the Autumnal Equinox, a powerful time for witchcraft and spell casting. We believed the idea was to get me out of the way, and then they could work on Paul without my interference. I strongly suspected Riana was competitive and did not like to lose. She saw her defeat as a challenge and she had to win at any cost. I was viewed as a threat.

145

Unfortunately, for them, they had no idea that the power keeping Paul from them was God, and not me.

Paul went to work and that morning I felt like I was in a trance. I could not study or motivate myself to do anything. I was in a zombie-like stupor. I knew something was wrong, and I had that familiar "pang" in my stomach that I always experienced when there was demonic activity around me. As I was in this paralyzing trance, the Scripture came to me, "No weapon formed against me shall prosper (Isaiah 54:17)." I had to keep reciting this verse over again in my mind. I was nauseas and dizzy for no apparent reason.

In the early morning hours of the next day, I woke up with two Scriptures repeating inside my mind. The first was, "No weapon formed against you shall prosper," and the second was, "Greater is He that is in you than he who is in the world (1John 4:4)." Even upon waking, these verses continually repeated in my mind. I had this feeling of impending doom, but did not know why. I knew I had to cling to the Scriptures that the Lord had given me, and that was what I did.

I had to be alert. I knew that Satan roamed around like a roaring lion seeking someone to devour (1Peter 5:8). I received an Email from a friend who reminded me to "put on the whole armor of God and stand" (obey) because the battle belongs to the Lord (Ephesians 6:10). Interestingly, in Paul's therapy session the counselor gave him the same Scripture verse. It seemed like a showdown was about to take place.

That evening I spoke with Paul about the events in my life, and he agreed that I had to be highly vigilant for demonic attack. As I talked with him, I could feel that demonic heat on the back of my head. This was another sign I developed to sense the presence of evil near me. I kept getting thoughts like voices in my head telling me that I was getting sick, but the Holy Spirit interjected and said, "You are not getting sick because by His stripes you are healed (Isaiah 53:3)."

Additionally, I kept hearing voices inside my head telling me that Paul was keeping a secret from me; that he had plans to leave me. I recognized the spirit of fear wanting to gain control. I knew that I had to expose the lies that the enemy wanted to sow in my heart. Therefore, I told Paul about the thoughts. Paul assured me that he had no plans to leave. He said he could be deceitful in many areas, but could not fake his relationship with Christ. For the first time in a long while, he felt free because he had no secrets. After our conversation, the deceiving thoughts and the spirit of fear dissipated.

That evening as I was getting ready for school, I noticed numerous large red ants in my bathroom sink. I could not see from where they were coming. There was no originating "ant line." They would just appear. It was interesting for the fact that we have never had an ant problem in our house, much less swarming red ants inside my white bathroom sink. One ant bit me and it hurt. I began to feel dizzy again and fear came upon me. Yet, God kept reassuring me not to be afraid.

I contacted Paul as he was coming home from work. He said that he received another priority mail package from Riana. He immediately threw it in the shredder with no reluctance. Obedience to God's commands would keep him safe. So, what was happening to me? I felt overwhelmed, tired, and depressed. There was so much going on and no time for rest. I was frustrated.

The next day was Thursday exactly thirteen weeks to the exact day since Paul's rescue. It was also the Autumnal Equinox. I cannot be certain that the number thirteen and Equinox had any significance, but something very strange happened to me.

As I was getting ready to meet a girlfriend to see a movie, I noticed my white robe that I had hanging on the closet door was covered with the same type of large red ants that I had seen in my bathroom sink. They were numerous and very noticeable. They were scurrying on the outside. They appeared frantic. There was no pattern to wandering. They were running into each other and going off in different directions. I have never seen ants behave this way.

I also noticed three odd things. The first thing I noticed was, that this particular robe was the robe Paul had bought me from the hotel that he was rescued from. The second thing I noticed was my other robe hanging next to the white one was unaffected. Not one ant was found on that one. And the last oddity was that, once again there was no "ant trail" anywhere, not on the floor and not on the ceiling. I could not find from where they were coming. So, where did they come from? This was significant.

When Paul had called me, I told him about the ants on my white robe. He agreed that this was a strange phenomenon. The color red was a clear warning of danger. Before I left the house, I put both robes in the washing machine. I went to my closet to check for more ants, and there were not any in sight. Not even one. So, where did they go?

Demonization vs. Possession

Before going on to the next portion of our story, there are things that we need to clarify and explain to the reader. What you are about to read is disturbing and perplexing, but they occurred and we write the truth. First, allow us to take you on a side trip about the workings and origins of demons. Second, this background will assist you in understanding what happened to us next. This book is not going to go into detail about the nuances of demon "possession" because there are many great books and authors who have tackled this subject very clearly.

Suffice it to say, the term "demonic possession" often conjures up images of a person totally in a trance and unable to control any behaviors, much like a robot. Our modern day Western mind envisions a person under the total control of demons, and literally owned or possessed by them acting much like a zombie.

Perhaps this is the case when people are demonically insane. The New Testament Greek uses a word translated "demon possessed." The accounts of these "possessed people" relate to them as demonized, under the influence of a demon(s), under the power of a demon(s). They are oppressed, tormented, sickened, or controlled, but not a total unaware robot zombie possessed by an unclean spirit.

To a very real extent, we are all influenced, harassed, sickened, and tormented by demonic spirits at different times and depths. It all depends on our willingness to allow the Holy Spirit to sanctify us by dropping these things from our fallen human natures. Demonization can occur whenever Christians indulge in willful rebellious sin and evil imaginations. God's hedge of protection may be breeched at these times of open disobedience. But, when a Christian is walking in the Spirit (not in their soul nature), yielding their lives totally to God, they are protected by the blood sacrifice of our Lord Jesus Christ. They are warriors fighting this spiritual war. A Christian's spirit cannot be demon possessed.

Yes, Christians walking in the Spirit are tempted by evil forces to sin. They are always subject to the demonic attack of deception, which attempts to get Christians to think wrongly and entertain evil imaginations. Thereby, opening up a door for demons to come in and harass them. Christians are tested and tried in these areas, but this is not the same as being "demonized."

Trials and tribulations are a necessary part of spiritual growth and maturity, but being demonized is pure torment, harassment or illness due to some breech in the protective hedge on the Christian's part. The Holy Spirit will have to reveal the areas in a person's personality that need repair, and close those open doors and holes in the wall. This is sanctification, and being made perfect in Christ.

The verses in Ecclesiastes 10:8 teaches us, "A serpent may bite him who breaks through a wall." If a Christian breaks through the protective hedge of the blood of Christ by rebellious sin, a serpent or demon may attach to them physically for illness or psychically (soul) for mental and emotional issues. Ephesians 4:22, 23, 24 - 27 declares, "Lay aside your old self, which is corrupted in accordance with the lusts of deceit. Be renewed in the *SPIRIT* of your mind. Put on the new self in the likeness of God. Do not give the devil an opportunity." Clearly, Christians can do the opposite. They can give the devil an opportunity to demonize them if they refuse to be renewed in the *SPIRIT* of their mind, continue in their old fleshly (soul) self, and refuse to put on the nature of God.

Even good Christians must be alert for Satan's deceptions and attacks. They are not exempt in this area. "Be sober in spirit, be on the alert. Your adversary, the devil prowls around like a roaring lion, seeking someone to devour." Being sober in spirit and alert for your enemy is a command given to us through the Apostle Peter in 1Peter 5:8.

In summary, there are people, unsaved people, who willingly give up control to demonic spirits in certain areas of their lives. Some types of mental and physical illnesses, emotional and spiritual maladies are the result of such behaviors but not all. There also are people who are Christians justified in the blood of Christ. They are going through a sanctification process where God reveals to them in due time certain ungodly and unholy characteristics of their personality. With repentance, these ugly spirits are expelled away from them, and their influence and control are broken. God will give deliverance and healing.

Christians can certainly be demonized. All Christians fight their fallen nature in the struggle and goal of perfection in Christ. Often, demonic strongholds and curses are a part of our fallen condition, and they have to be expelled from the Christian's "soul" nature. Not that the Christian is demon possessed rather they are under the influence, control, and power of evil forces working inside their human fleshly nature. The Holy Spirit resides in the Christian's spirit, and works to cleanse the Christian's soul or human nature. Demonic forces never operate in the area of a Christian's spirit. That is where the Holy Spirit dwells.

The Apostle Paul wrote to the church of the Thessalonians, "Now may the God of peace himself *SANCTIFY* you completely, and may your whole *spirit, body, and soul* be preserved blameless at the coming of our Lord Jesus Christ. (1Thessalonians 5:23)." It is the Holy Spirit residing in your spirit, which *sanctifies* the Christian. He loosens and drops those evil inclinations of sin and carnal nature through the sanctification process. This process is according to the will of God, but also depends on the Christian's willingness to submit more to the Spirit of Christ inside of him, and less to the evil human nature within his own soul.

In 2Timothy 2:20 and 21, the Apostle Paul tells us that there are both vessels of honor and dishonor within the house of God or the church. He declares that, "If anyone cleanses himself from the latter (being a vessel of dishonor), he will be a vessel for honor, *SANCTIFIED* and useful for the Master, prepared for every good work." How is a Christian cleansed to become a vessel for honor for God's work? The Christian is cleansed as they yield to the Holy Spirit residing within their spirit to be transformed into the image of Christ. This is sanctification. This is putting off the old (soul) nature.

Many Christians suffer from physical illnesses, which the medical profession cannot diagnose or properly treat. These illnesses just appear, and are not rooted in a cause. Such illnesses are often associated with demonic attack on the Christian's body. Sins not confessed with lack of forgiveness are just some of the open doors that can cause such an attack.

Additionally, not understanding or fully believing in the authority we have in Christ over demonic attack can result in our lack of victory and healing, because we do not exercise our rightful authority over these things. Read the Gospel of Mark. Right from the start of Christ's ministry, often he was expelling demons associated with illness. When a person is healed, they may also be freed from demonization. Often, but not always, physical sickness and demonization go hand in hand.

Origin of Demons

This is a topic for another book. There is too much teaching on this subject to place here. We will give a brief summary of the origin of your enemies. Most people have not been taught the origin of demons or unclean spirits, and so by not knowing what they are and what they were, we misunderstand how they operate to destroy a human life. Again, this is not the topic of this book, but suffice it to say that demons are "disembodied spirits." They used to have a body and now they do not.

In Genesis 6, the account of the "watchers" or fallen angels mating with humans is recorded. Also, great insight is gained through the ancient books of Enoch and Jubilees. The Christian interested in studying further must read these books for what they are worth. This union of angel and human produced a "hybrid" creature, part angel and part human, and they were strong, vicious, kings of the earth consuming human resources. These were the "gods" of ancient myths and legends.

They were also evil continually, and taught humans the art of war, spell casting, enchantments, beautification, pride, and all witchcraft among other things. These children of the angels literally corrupted the human race along with many of the animals. Noah and his family of eight were found genetically pure, uncorrupted by the mixing of angel and human. They were to repopulate the earth with humans.

After the flood destroyed this corrupted species, God made a covenant to never destroy the earth again with water. However, according to the Book of Enoch, another set of Watchers (angels assigned to watch over mankind) committed the exact sin of rebellion as their first counterparts. God made another provision to save his creation by becoming flesh in the man/God Jesus Christ to redeem mankind from these evil spirits.

The Nephilim cannot be saved because they are part immortal (angel) and part mortal (human). So when God destroyed their physical bodies in the flood of Noah, their immortal spirits became disembodied. They cannot resurrect or take part in the salvation of Christ. They are bound to this earth, and are known as "earth spirits." They remain this way until the future final judgment and consummation of all things by God. Then they will be destroyed. This is why they must control and influence a human body to continue to live out their lust and greed.

Notice the people in the New Testament had not questioned the existence of evil spirits (demons). What they questioned and were amazed over was finally a human (Jesus) had actual authority over unclean spirits (Mark 1:27). The very fact that Jesus had authority over demons was a sign that the Kingdom of God was at hand and very near (Matthew 12:28).

155

These disembodied spirits of angel/human hybrids know that they will be destroyed on the Lord's final day of judgment. In Matthew 8:29, the demons ask Jesus, "Have you come here to torment us before *the time*?" In an unrelated account in Mark 1:24, demons speaking through a man in the Jewish Synagogue asked Jesus the same question. "Let us alone! What have we to do with You, Jesus of Nazareth? Did You come to *destroy* us? I know who You are, the Holy One of God!"

But until then, they are allowed to assist Satan (the original fallen angel) in rebellion against God, and in his testing of the human species. Satan and his fallen angels are not demons or disembodied earth spirits. They are the rulers and ancient powers of the air and near heavens. They use their "sons," the disembodied Nephilim to destroy the human race, which they hate.

According to the Book of Enoch and Jubilees, two hundred fallen angels or "Watchers" mated with humans before the flood of Noah. These are bound by the commandment of God in a place called Tartarus (Jude 1:6 and 2Peter 2:4) awaiting judgment. However, there was a second group of Watchers who did the exact same thing after the flood (Genesis 6:4). Their children or hybrid offspring became the giants, mighty warriors, and unclean people. The nation of Israel needed to destroy these idol worshipers by the command of God while taking over the Promised Land in Canaan. This is one reason they were forbidden to marry or intermingle their seed with them. The second group of Watchers is not bound in Tartarus, but occupy the air space above earth as principalities, rulers and powers of the air (Ephesians 6:12).

Demons have "demonized" humans from after the flood of Noah. If you want to see how they attack you, read the stories regarding the tactics, techniques, and warfare of ancient Israel's enemies. This is how they attack you today. Christians are attacked all the time. Often, these spirits get "into" and latch onto a physical part of the body or the "soul" nature of a person to create all kinds of havoc physically and mentally if that person has an open door or breech in their Godly protection. Perhaps they have not put on the whole armor of God as stated in Ephesians 6. This is why spiritual warfare is essential. Only through the authority given the Christian through Christ Jesus can the Christian expel these evil forces from their life. Sadly, many Christians do not understand this, and so suffer needlessly through demonic torment in some way or another.

We pray you will understand the nature and origin of demons and evil spirits better now. We had to take this brief side trip in order to fully explain what happened to us next. If we had not taken this side trip, then the following account may have been too shocking on the reader's senses. Now you realize a Christian can be "demonized," oppressed, harassed, sickened, and tormented in their "soul" human nature. However, a Christian's spirit cannot be possessed. Prayerfully, the following account will make sense to you.

Personal Demons

157

This brings me (Linda) back to the red ants on my robe incident. Recall that both Paul and I felt that this was a severe warning sign to us that something bad was about to take place. Recall, first there were mysterious red ants in my kitchen sink. One bit me. Second, I had the same mysterious red ants on my white robe.

That same evening (thirteen weeks since Paul's rescue, and on the Autumnal Equinox), I was going with Paul to a police academy graduation. Some of the recruits he had hired were now graduating, and the various police departments involved in the academy training always put on a big show in a graduation ceremony for the families and recruits.

Paul was always different in police uniform. When he had on his badge and gun, he would not hold my hand or show any display of affection because he thought this was presenting an unprofessional appearance. But, this particular night that rule of his would really get to me and push my buttons. I was raw, tired, and feeling overwhelmed in many areas of my life. My marriage, my grades, my school attendance, and my spiritual walk were all taking their toll on me.

I met Paul at his office, he changed into his police uniform and we left for the graduation. He told me that he did not want his two worlds to collide, meaning he did not want conflict because his marriage (me) and his work to be co-joined for the evening. This is what he used to say to me when he was seeing Riana. This statement hurt my feelings, but I just brushed it off.

Arriving at the auditorium, Paul told me not to hold his hand in public. I knew his rules, but this time they really upset me. As we walked to the door, he again reminded me not to hold his hand. Now, this time I really became irritated with Paul. I snapped back and told him that I was well aware of his rules and that he was annoying me because he kept on nagging me. Then he said that my reaction aggravated him, and that he hated our new open communication policy.

His comment closed my heart. I was highly infuriated by now. I thought, "See, he has not changed. God delivered him, he is feeling good, and now he is acting like before. He does not appreciate me. He is using me." Paul's behavior aggravated me more. This was the little crack in which my enemy entered, and would later bring chaos and havoc into our lives.

After the ceremony, we went out to eat and everything was fine. We held hands and had an enjoyable evening. I did not have any harsh feelings toward Paul, and my aggravation disappeared. We went home and fell asleep, but there was a crack in my armor and the enemy was about to pounce like a roaring lion. We would later learn from this experience that certain "soul" personality traits had to be purged from me for our marriage relationship to completely heal. So, what Satan intended for harm to us, God used as a cleansing.

Unclean Spirits Speak

That night as we slept unbeknownst to us, a very dark occurrence was about to take place. Only by the grace of our God were we able to survive such an ordeal. Later, I discovered that at 1:30 AM, Paul's mother was awakened from sleep and began praying for us. Then, at 2:17 AM, at our house, I felt this intense heat inside of me. I was burning up inside. It felt like a fire was lit within me. I was groaning and thrashing about as Paul attempted to wake me. I could not wake up. I was on fire and I could not come out of my sleep. I could not open my eyes, but inside I was aware and conscious of what was happening.

I saw a woman hanging from a noose. It was me! With my eyes still closed, I told Paul that I was sad because he did not love me, he had not changed, he did not want to hold my hand that night, I shut down, and I was hurt. All this was going through my mind, but I could not wake up. I started to cry. Paul gently touched my forehead and said that it was a lie from Satan. "Wake up, Linda!" he yelled. He tried to physically sit me up in bed. I was like a rag doll. I told him, "You do not love me." Paul exclaimed, "That is a lie."

Suddenly, this mocking spirit came forth from me and said to Paul, "You would not hold her hand last night." Paul rebuked the demon, but it sneered at him and said, "She does not believe you." For two hours, Paul prayed, read Scriptures, rebuked the spirits, and tried to talk with me, but nothing was pushing me through to deliverance.

After several hours, I told Paul that I was all right. Yet, when he asked me to look at him, I could not have eye contact with him. He knew the spirits were still on me.

Then I would mockingly laugh with the laughter turning into wailing and sobbing. I felt so tormented inside. I would cry out to my dead mother for relief. Paul commanded that I cry out to Jesus, but when I tried, I would continue to call upon my dead mother.

I felt another spirit push forward from inside of me. This was a masculine, defiant spirit that mocked Paul. When Paul had me read aloud Psalm 23, all I could eek out was "the Lord is my shepherd" before this mocking spirit would laugh in a sinister manner.

I laid down on the bed in a seductive manner, exposed and seductively invited him to come to me. Paul later told me that I was laughing and looking at him, but he knew it was not me. He later said that this was the most eerie and frightening part for him because I looked exactly liked Riana when I was attempting to seduce him. Paul quickly rebuked the spirit in the Name of Jesus. I would begin wailing again. I do not remember doing these things, but Paul would later recount that "I was gone," and whatever was controlling me was not his wife. He recounted that the look in my eyes that told him I was gone, frightened him.

Remember, that Paul had just submitted his life to God in a meaningful way just one week earlier. He was a new Christian. He had no experience at all dealing with demons manifesting in a person, let alone his wife. He felt like it was either sink or swim for him. He felt like God just tossed him into the deep end to test his survival instincts. This was a horrible and frightening experience for the both of us.

At his wit's end, Paul telephoned his mother who happened to be up at this time of night praying over us. In the background, she could hear me wailing at the top of my lungs, and she knew it was evil. I stopped crying and became stoic in expression. Paul told me to get dressed because we were going to his mother's house so the both of them could pray this demon from me.

Surprisingly, I obeyed but moved around in a daze. I got into the car and felt myself going in and out mentally. Paul said that I would have a great deliverance, but I just snickered and said, "Whatever." On the way to his mother's house, Paul would talk about the blood of Christ and I would grimace and growl. The defiant mocking spirit wanted me to challenge Paul to play his rock music, specifically a band that had much magical influence on him in the recent past. But, I would not allow it to use my mouth.

On my mother-in-law's couch, my head jerked back with my eyes rolling back into their sockets, and I would mock and laugh at their prayers. Both Paul and his mother began speaking in tongues and praying fervently in the Spirit of Christ. As my head thrashed forward and backward, my eyeballs rolled back and my spirit saw Jesus. I remember I said, "He is my Jesus. He is my Jesus." I reached my right hand toward the ceiling while God was filling me with His Holy Spirit. I cried out, "Jesus, do not leave me!" I knew he would never leave me nor forsake me, but I was in a place I did not want to be in, and I did not want to be left there.

As I cried out, "Jesus, do not leave me," I screamed a horrifying scream. It was the demons leaving me. I felt them leave. They were no longer attached to my psyche or soul. Paul later told me it sounded like a large wounded animal coming from my vocal cords. It scared me because I knew the sound coming from me was not my voice, or anything I could reproduce. I started praising God and speaking in tongues. I felt such a release.

This was a ghastly experience. It was now 5:00 AM, as we left my mother-in-law's house. This was much more than oppression by an evil spirit. Yet, the spirits could not totally control me. I was so glad I was able to get into the car with Paul and go to his mother's house for additional prayer. Also, I could not physically fight with, or escape from Paul, I only gave a lot of "lip" to him. It felt as if the spirits were "pushing" on me from inside rather than oppressing from outside. They were not in complete control over me.

Needless to say, this was a life-changing incident for Paul. He realized that he needed to always have the armor of God applied in his life. He felt that had he not been under God's umbrella, he would not have been able to expel the demons from me. He understood that spiritual warfare is an ongoing activity and being ready to fight is crucial for survival. Although, it seemed at times we were drowning, God was always in control.

A few days later, we had Paul's mother and one of his sisters come to our house and pray over every room. As we walked from place to place, God would point out

163

books or items that we needed to destroy. Paul threw away all his Masonic books, apron, rings, and jewelry. I threw away books I had not even read yet. The hardest things to destroy were years of journals that I had written, which were based on lies.

This was the beginning of several cleansings in our home. The cleansings still go on to this day. Whenever God's Spirit points to something we should destroy, He tells us so. The Holy Spirit will reveal to you in His time the things that must go. We have burned writings in the fireplace, thrown books into the trash, shredded documents, and destroyed other items by smashing them apart. The important thing to remember is to flow with God's direction and be obedient in getting rid of occult or binding items in your home. Some items may have emotional significance, and you may not want to get rid of them, but you must listen to the Lord and get rid of them. Especially, if you find that you have a very strong attachment to them.

One of the other things we did to strengthen our "spiritual muscles" was to "FAST" television, movies, music, or anything that was not of God. Instead of "fasting" food, we deprived our natural desires and lusts of the things of this world. By reducing the carnal person, we increased the spiritual person inside. It is amazing how much the world influences our thinking. Just removing yourself from television and entertainment while focusing on Scripture, prayer and Godly things will increase your spiritual growth exponentially.

They Linger

Satan and his army are defeated (present tense) by Christ and awaiting their final dissolution. If they can keep you from believing that fact, then they will continue to operate as if they have a right to do so in your life. Paul and I were getting stronger in the Lord, but had so much to learn about our enemy and his tactics. The Lord was faithful to teach us through practical, hands on training.

One day, the Lord taught us how cunning the enemy's deceptions can be. How the enemy can use the transference of spirits from one person to another in order to appear to be omnipresent. Of course, we know that Satan is not omnipresent, but only God is. This is how the lesson unfolded. On this particular day, Paul and I were at home working on our individual projects. I was in the study doing some homework when Paul entered the room. During our conversation, I began to feel irritated with him because he was interrupting my studies. I felt he did not care about what I was doing, which led to feeling sorry for myself, which led to feeling guilty on account of my irritation. When Paul detected my irritation from my facial expressions, he became offended and walked away. I then felt more guilt and anger, which resulted in feeling depressed and discouraged. I prayed, and I knew I had to ask Paul for his forgiveness. I went looking for him. When I found him, I told him I was sorry.

Things went along fine after that, but then I noticed his demeanor changed and he appeared irritated with me.

He felt anger and discouragement. This teeter-totter exchange between us was occurring too often to be normal. Something was wrong. Paul and I are not that thin skinned with each other. In fact, we enjoy each other's company.

Paul and I prayed and asked the Lord what was happening. He opened our spiritual eyes and we were able to "see" that there was an evil spirit that was allowed to influence us. This imp kept transferring between the two of us so fast that at one point it appeared that we were both demonically attacked at the same time. By shifting so quickly between the two of us, it tried to convince us it was omnipresent like our God! Its purpose was to give the illusion that we were both discouraged at the same time, leaving no strong spouse to uplift the other. Once the Lord revealed the enemy's deceptive scheme, we were able to rebuke the evil spirit in the authority of Jesus our Lord.

That same night we had a special invitation to attend a New Members meeting at our pastor's house. It would be the first step in joining and becoming involved in the church. We surmised that Satan did not want us at this meeting. It would not be in his best interest if we were to be involved in a Spirit-filled church and becoming acquainted with other believers. Later it became apparent to us that the battle we fought earlier was also designed to prevent our attending this meeting. However, God's will prevailed and, we went.

This whole ordeal was so time consuming that my school grades were suffering. I wanted to quit so badly.

166

Yet, God kept on telling me to trust in Him. I would become so discouraged and depressed thinking about my classes and upcoming tests that I was ripe for exposure to the demonic lies that would soon creep in.

Remember, Paul was doing fine by this time, and he was growing in faith. But, I started to feel left behind, unappreciated, and unloved. I thought, "I did all this work and sacrifice for Paul. Why are not things working out for me? Why am I struggling?" I began to build up walls and close my heart from Paul because I felt I had no place in his world and he only cared about himself.

Satan was using my past hurt and rejection to hinder me from fully walking in faith and trust in the Lord. Yet, the Lord would continue to encourage me to "trust" Him. One morning, I felt so tired and discouraged. School was taking its toll on me. My marriage and personal life were weighing me down. I needed some relief, so I had decided to quit my studies. However, in my alone time with the Lord, I thought He was telling me to hold on, do not quit. But how could I be certain it was Him? I asked the Lord for a sign. I said, "Lord, if this is from You, then have Paul call me today and ask how I am doing." Sure enough, Paul called and asked how I was doing! I was so excited that I told Paul about my fleece to the Lord. The Lord revealed to Paul how the enemy was deceiving me. When he explained how Satan was using the lies against me, I gained a new resolve to trust the Lord in everything, including school.

We learned that Satan does not fight fair and he is an opportunist. He looks for opportunities to attack when we are most vulnerable. And we are most vulnerable when we are too busy to pray. When we neglect time with the Lord in prayer and Bible study, we expose ourselves to the satanic arsenal. When we do not make time to spend with the Lord and study His Word before a satanic assault, we will most likely not take the time to pray to the Lord during or after a satanic assault. That is when we are vulnerable to Satan infiltrating our "soul" mind with lies and deceit. Do not let too much time lapse before you do stop and pray against his attacks. Remember, our enemy does not fight fair and he is an opportunist.

Another way that Satan and his minions operate is through modern technology. We have many examples of this. For example, there were numerous times when we would send text messages or telephone calls to each other, and the receiving party would not get the message. These messages were of encouragement or support, but they would get "lost" in cyber space strangely enough.

Satan also uses our past to design future temptations to entice us. Here is a story of how Satan used modern technology, a potential female recruit, and sexual enticement to tempt Paul. It was during the time that Paul was in charge of a police bureau, which recruited and hired police department employees, and recruiting females was a high priority for the department. A few years earlier, Paul met and befriended a female security guard who wanted to become a police officer. He directed her to his staff to assist her with the hiring process. That was the extent of his involvement with her.

Then, one particular day, while Paul was at work, this female telephoned him out-of-the-blue and told him that she had a strong desire to send him a provocative Email. Paul was shocked by this statement, and asked her why in the world would she say that? She related that while she was at work and bored, she began to think about him in a sensual way. Paul replied to her, "An idle mind is the devil's workshop." He told her that he was never interested in her, and was not flattered by her flirtations. She left the conversation saying, "Well, let's get a drink sometime." He never heard from her again.

Because Paul and I learned that we should not have any secrets between us, he shared the incident with me. No doubt, this scenario was designed and delivered from the pit of Hell. The Lord was using these tests and trials of faith and trust to train us to become warriors in His army. Each test and every trial was allowed by the Lord to strengthen us in Him. As we read the Word of God and prayed, the Lord taught us how to apply His truth to our life situations. It was real life experience and not only book learning. These trials of discipline sharpen our spiritual discernment skills, and teach us how to recognize and use our spiritual gifts.

The Training of Faith

We had a conversation about God training us to walk by faith and not by sight. But, I (Paul) did not expect to have a "lesson" the next day. This is the story of extreme vertigo, a demonic dizziness that attacked Linda and I on several occasions, but this first one was the worst I had experienced.

In the early morning hours, on a day I had a major presentation to give at work, I was struck with a debilitating dizziness. There was a department-wide mandatory meeting, and I was giving an update on my division to about 1,000 people at 8:00 AM. It was a very serious and important presentation. I had to give it.

Around 1:30 AM, I woke up to extreme vertigo. The whole room was spinning and it was making me nauseas. It was the strangest feeling. No matter if my eyes were open or closed, I felt everything moving and spinning around me. I had to wake up at 5:00 AM, but I could not sleep because of the vertigo. I prayed and prayed, but it would not leave me. I woke Linda to pray for me, but the dizziness would not subside.

I stayed awake, and when I finally left the bed to get ready, I could hardly move. I could not walk. It was like being on board a ship tossed back and forth on the ocean accompanied with the resulting motion sickness. Linda prayed over me again, and the Lord told her to tell me, "To go about my business and to trust Him. The dizziness would be released, but not right away." Interestingly enough this was the same thing God told me while I was praying earlier. There was a battle going on with God fighting it, and I just needed to trust in Him and have faith in His promise.

I became frustrated. I was so sick and nauseas I began to cry. I told God, "This is not a good day for a test or a lesson in faith." As I bounced off the walls to get to my car, I was afraid I would not be able to drive. I could barely see. My eyes saw double vision, and I was so sick to my stomach.

I inched down my driveway, and after traveling just a few yards I had to stop, open the car door, and vomit. I did this several times just leaving my driveway. I knew the presentation was going to be a disaster. I was only worried about vomiting in front of a 1,000 onlookers.

"God, God, why?" I cried. I drove the car leaning on the center console for an hour with one eye open and barely made it to my destination. I could not eat or drink. I just needed to lie down. But, the Spirit inside me kept saying, "Trust in the Lord. It is not by sight but by faith." The Spirit inside directed me to another road to travel to the auditorium, and at first I argued, then gave it a try. It was the right road because I was able to drive slowly and safely.

I arrived and could hardly stand, so I sat down right away. People and co-workers were milling about before the start of the meeting. They had coffee and pastries, and it all was making me more ill. They would walk up to me and begin conversing. I just knew I must look like "Hell." I had not slept, eaten, or drank anything. I was sick to my stomach, and I had vomited earlier. I felt like death.

But, the strangest thing happened. Everyone kept telling me how "good I looked." It was obvious to me that what they were seeing on the outside, was not what I was feeling on the inside. I would tell them how sick I was, and they would tell me that I never looked better. This had to be Christ in me.

I limped up to the podium and opened my mouth. God was merciful, and I gave the presentation without incident. It was about noon, before I started feeling better and could eat. It was a lesson in faith. It is not what you "see" or what you "feel" rather it is what you "know." I saw (and felt) illness, but knew God was there for me in this trial. Others just saw the power of Christ, and never knew how sick I felt. It was amazing.

I worked late into the evening as usual. I drove straight from work for about an hour to a church near my home. I was hungry because I had not eaten much due to my earlier vertigo. I wanted a hamburger, but time was cut short before the church service started. The Spirit inside me said, "Crucify your flesh." What? I was hungry and wanted a hamburger first, and then I would go to church.

I saw a fast food drive thru restaurant, and decided to pull in. There was a long line. I knew if I stayed in line, I would certainly be late for church. The Spirit said, "Crucify the flesh." I had such a long bad day, and now this. So, I made a decision to go to church. I backed out of line and went to church remembering that they had bags of potato chips for sale in the courtyard. I remember seeing these bags of chips, and so I thought, "I'll just pick up a couple of bags and woof down some chips before service."

I arrived at church, got my seat, and then decided to feed my flesh with some potato chips. I walked out into the courtyard toward these shiny cellophane bags. To my surprise and disappointment, the bags were of coffee, not potato chips. With my crucified flesh, I enjoyed a conversation with a nice couple I met, and my hunger left me. I participated in a communion service and God blessed me with His Word.

Things started changing for the better for us. Our testing and trials were meant for spiritual growth and training rather than from rebellion and disobedience. We would be remiss to tell you that everything went back to normal and we had no more demonic attacks and disappointments in life. There were (and still are) many things occurring we do not fully understand. It has taken a long time to drop many of our demonic strongholds from our personalities and soul natures. But, the Holy Spirit is continually sanctifying us.

We now would like to shift our focus on two spiritual concepts. First, you must understand our enemy in order to better combat his tactics. Second, learn how to defeat the enemy through Christ.

Chapter 10: Understanding Your Enemy

The Satanic Triangle

We are left with our carnal or natural man to guide us through the difficulties of life when we do not commune with God through prayer and Scripture saturation, and when we do not submit to God's authority. Also, we have no guidance when we continue to practice sin, and refuse to allow the Holy Spirit to transform our lives. Having just ourselves to rely on, we then begin looking for the answers to our difficulties within this world system. The world system is controlled by your enemy, which uses deception to trick you into compromising your marriage in Christ. This little cocktail ignites when three angles merge to form the satanic triangle. Understanding how this triangle works and recognizing it when it comes to play is essential in your combat training.

The "flesh" is one side of the triangle. It is our natural or carnal person with all of its desires for pride, greed, hate, envy, strife, and all other natural personal characteristics. This flesh is pressed upon by the "world." The world is another side of this triangle, and it consists of Satan's world systems and philosophies. The world surrounds us with its violence, illicit sex, anger, racism, arrogance, lies, and other satanic characteristics. The system of the world is everywhere and one cannot escape it in the flesh. We live in a fallen world. In fact, the flesh desires the world and all it has to offer. People are carried away by the flesh and by the world if they are not re-born and renewed in the Spirit of God. Then it is an easy thing for "Satan," the final side of the triangle, to consume their lives with torment, destruction, lies and blindness. Eventually, people are led to ruin and finally eternal death.

Let us examine a Spiritual principle in Scripture regarding this satanic triangle. The following account is taken from the Gospel of Mark 4:15-20 (NKJV). Jesus had just finished telling a parable of "seeding and sowing," when His disciples asked Him to explain it to them. Jesus explains the seed's final destination, "And these are the ones by the wayside where the Word is sown. When they hear, Satan comes immediately and takes away the Word that was sown in their hearts."

Satan does this and this is the Satan side of the triangle. "Immediately," Satan steals the Word of God from your heart. There is no time lag here. This is the work of Satan, and results in the rejection of the Word of God that would bring you into obedience to Him. Do not make the mistake that this refers only to the unsaved sinner. It refers to you, the Christian. And, do not think this is a one-time occurrence.

This attempted stealing of the Word of God by Satan can happen everyday of your life. Every time you or your spouse lack faith in God's promises, His redemptive work, or in His Scriptures, then Satan has taken that seed away. Every time you just do not have the time to study God's Word with your spouse is when Satan steals it from you. Every time you place an idol (career, car, house, money, children, church service, television, Internet, etc.) before God, Satan has stolen the Word from you. If you continue to sin, you do not have the Word of God in you.

Therefore, the very first rule to understand is to have absolute knowledge that Satan is the enemy of your marriage and will steal the Word of God from your marriage if you are not diligent in this area. Men, you must begin taking your rightful role as priest in the home. You must read and study Scripture so you can discuss with and impart to your marriage partner. Women, you must begin encouraging your husband to take this role. He needs to "cover" you and provide protection over you in the spiritual realm. Once he begins to act as priest of the home, you will gain respect for him. You both equally share in Christ Jesus, however the Father is the head of Christ, Christ is the head of His called-out-ones, and husbands are the head of their house. Men, you are called to be priests, not kings and tyrants.

Paul and I (Linda) had many things in common, but the one thing that we did not share was in our relationship to God. I enjoyed going to church and being with other believers. Paul on the other hand, did not enjoy going to church. He definitely did not enjoy being with other people, much less Christians. Therefore, spiritually I felt alone. I longed for our spiritual life to be different, more in-sync. Because our spiritual differences, for years my husband did not "cover" me or act as priest of our home. He could not because he was not submitted to our Lord Jesus Christ, and therefore I could not be submitted under my husband. The majority of times I attended church and Bible studies alone. Although Paul had education in Biblical studies, he never was interested in growing spiritually with me. What we did not realize is that without the root of Christ in our marriage, we had no firm foundation. There was no foundation based on ultimate truth, and so if Paul could be deceived and led astray, I could also be made to believe satanic lies and doctrines of demons.

Paul was living his own life out of the presence of God, and this left me alone to fight demonic deceptions, depression, illness, and mental torment. I had no one to pray over me, to uphold me before the throne of God, and no one to be accountable to. I was living for God the best I knew how, and I was doing it solo. Therefore, when Paul became demonized, and under the spell of witchcraft, it affected me in a horrible way.

Again, let us stress the fact that Satan wants to steal God's Word from your marriage. You must fight to prevent this from occurring. Getting back to the Gospel of Mark, let us look at the flesh side of the triangle. Jesus continues to answer the question about the seeds, "These likewise are the ones sown on stony ground who, when they hear the Word, immediately receive it with gladness; and they have no root in themselves, and so endure only for a time. Afterward, when tribulation or persecution arises for the Word's sake, immediately they stumble."

The flesh does this and this is the flesh side of the triangle. You or your spouse may be hearing the Word of God right now, but because of your own doubt, pride, fear, self-righteousness, self-pity, or self-centered nature, you will lose the zeal when trouble comes. Yes, at first you give God your best and make all sorts of promises to Him to live right in His sight. But, because you lack character within, because you have no root in yourself, you stumble and fall away at the first hint of trouble caused by your new beliefs. Notice the Word does not say, "No root in the church, family, America, etc." The Word says, "No root in themselves." This is a character issue. It is an issue of maturity. Are you a coward or a warrior?

When we firmly recommitted to God and made "Christ-like-ness" our main objective, that is when the trouble from Hell started. After experiencing many demonic manifestations, which drove us into spiritual growth, we just wanted to get back to normal and be common Sunday-go-to-church Christians and live life in peace. Well my friends, there is no such thing as a "normal" Christian. If you commit to holiness and quit sinning then God will grow you. Afflictions, troubles, and tribulations will push you and tug hard at the roots of your heart. This is the truth. Your character – not Satan's deceptions – is what is at stake here. You have to have the guts and inner strength to cry out to God and commit (repent) wholly and totally to Him for deliverance. If you are weak in character, you will never enter the battle. You have already been defeated by your enemy and taken captive.

We have examined the satanic triangle from the angle of Satan and from the angle of the sinful nature of humans. The last side of the triangle is the world angle. In explaining His parable, Jesus teaches, "Now these are the ones sown among thorns; they are the ones who hear the Word, and the cares of this world, the deceitfulness of riches, and the desires for other things entering in choke the Word, and it becomes unfruitful."

The world does this and this is the world side of the triangle. The world or the cares of the world choke out the good seed of the Word of God. This is related to the character issues above, but is different in that it comes from the outside rather then from the inside. The pressures from the outside world then cause the collapse of the inward character. The outside worldly concerns lead to greediness and short sightedness. You or your spouse may be in this situation. You have heard the Word (Satan had not snatched it from you), you have accepted it gladly (no weak character in the face of troubles), but you cannot produce any spiritual fruit in your marriage because you are too busy running around doing worthless things and being wrapped up in the cares of this world. World cares are idol worship. Anything or anyone you place ahead of God is an idol.

Linda will verify that I (Paul) spent years furthering my career and climbing the organizational ladder with ill intent. I wanted more money, more power, more authority, more praise and adoration. I placed my ambition over the will of God in my life. In fact, I never once considered inquiring of God about His will or purpose for me in my career. I had my life under control and I knew how much money I needed to make and how much power I wanted to exert. I never once considered how I might commingle my Christianity with my work. They were always separate (because I had no true Christianity). And, when you place your trust in something other than God, and it comes crashing down, you will come tumbling down also.

So, now let us look outside of the triangle and hear Jesus' final words on the topic, "But these are the ones sown on good ground, those who hear the Word, accept it, and bear fruit: some thirty-fold, some sixty, and some a hundred." Hopefully, this is the picture of your marriage. Both have heard, accepted, and produced God's Word through the fruit of the Spirit. Satan cannot steal it from you because you submit to God and resist the devil. Your inner character is strong in the Lord and you have learned to receive trials and afflictions with joy knowing that they produce "Christ-like-ness" in you. The world cannot press against your marriage because you are both eternal minded and not focused on temporal earthly lusts. And now you produce fruit and are used of God for His will and purpose.

Understanding how Satan uses human nature (the un-regenerated person) and his worldly system against your marriage is the first tool and weapon in your new arsenal for a Martial Marriage. Recognizing the unrelenting need to be bathed in the Word of God is essential for your effective combat. Your marriage needs the Sword of the Spirit to fight the enemy.

Quit Sinning

This is Paul writing. Listen, I intellectually bought into all sorts of "convenient" theologies and teachings that would release me from accountability. But here is the truth; a person can have a born again experience and then fall away from God in continued and practiced sin and will not enter into the Kingdom of Heaven. It is backsliding. We give this a new coat of paint and say that we are "out of fellowship" with God, "not walking" with the Lord now, or "not living in the fullness of Christ" for the time being. We have even heard this one, "I'm out of season." But, all this paint only masks the truth. The person that backslides (out of fellowship, not walking, not living, etc.) is in extreme danger of going to Hell if they do not repent. Yes, you are going to Hell because God is holy, and demands that we be holy (set apart, sanctified, obedient, submitted, etc.).

How can anyone expect to enter into His holy presence when not holy? Yes, we live under the grace and blood of Christ, but God's laws and requirements have not changed. It does not matter that you were "saved" once. You must continue in Christ to enter the Kingdom. We are not talking about making mistakes, but a lifestyle that continues to "practice" sin. If you do not hear anything else from our message, please hear this - quit sinning!

The most important thing you can do for your marriage is to stop practicing and participating in habitual sin. For the life of me I cannot understand why some preachers and theologians insist on arguing the case for "once saved, always saved," instead of recognizing the need for a repentant Christian being brought into holiness. Do not be deceived by a doctrine of demons, just quit sinning.

Jesus knew earthly-minded people would not enter into the Kingdom of Heaven. The "no compromise" language is used as He called the people to Himself, "Whoever desires to come after Me, let him deny himself, and take up his cross, and follow Me. For whoever desires to save his life will lose it, but whoever loses his life for My sake and the Gospel's will save it." Jesus then gave His "followers" four things they must do in order to enter Heaven.

1. Deny yourself (suffer in the world for the obedience to God).

2. Take up the cross (rejection for your "no compromise" beliefs in the Word of God).

3. Lose your life (die to your carnal nature, be killed in the flesh, put it on the cross).

4. Will save it (your spiritual man will resurrect when you put your flesh to death).

One cannot hang their hat on the fact that they once were saved. A person in a condition of perpetual sin without repentance - not denying their flesh, not taking up the cross, and not following Christ is a lost soul.

Additionally, Mark 9:43-50, is clear about sinning and entering into Heaven. Jesus said that if something is causing you to sin, then get rid of it no matter how painful it is. He said that it is better to enter in the Kingdom of God lame or blind then to go to Hell with eyes, hands, and feet. Christ did not say that if one's eye causes him to sin he should patch it up, hide it, ignore it, think positive about it, love it, bless it, share it with others, deny it, or any other nonsense. Christ said to pluck it out! If you are not willing to pluck out the things in your life that causes habitual sin, then you will enter into Hell.

The idea of practicing sin was one of my biggest downfalls in my marriage. I (Paul) thought of myself as a self-made shaman, a witch doctor or a sorcerer of sorts. Not realizing just how far I had traveled into occult practices, I believed myself spiritual. Keep in mind that I had still considered myself a "Christian!" Linda and I soon realized that there are many "Christians" who practice sin and they may be attending or serving in your church. Marriages are torn apart with secret disputes, anger, and violence that is hidden behind sealed doors painted white. Remember the story of the wealthy ruler who had it all including religion, but lacked just one thing. This one thing, which was lacking would prevent him from entering the Kingdom of Heaven.

While professing Christianity, I was filled with much anger, pride, and self centeredness. I never once thought of including God in major life-changing events.

Marriages, relationships, jobs, moves, and educational decisions were all made through my own intellect and wisdom. My own life was my idol. I trusted no man. I only trusted myself. I placed full confidence and reliability on my knowledge, skills, and abilities to obtain in life whatever I wanted regardless of the spiritual consequences. At one point in our lives, Linda and I had four mortgages and several rental properties. We owned new Harley Davidson motorcycles, and new cars. Our income increased and we spent freely on ourselves. There was nothing, within reason, that we could not buy. My confidence was on my purchasing power. I rocketed through my career in law enforcement, gaining a great reputation as a leader and as a "fast tracker."

I studied leadership philosophies from all manner of corporations and attended the leadership module developed by the West Point Military Academy. My self-confidence (faith and trust in myself only) propelled me to obtain a Master of Arts Degree in Behavioral Science, a second-degree black belt in Kung Fu, and become a published author with a book and several magazine articles. It seemed that I could accomplish whatever I set my mind to accomplish.

I worked hard and could solve any problem at my job. I was so efficient that I was selected and placed in key positions of power to effect change. My pride and love of self gave me the ability to compete fiercely. I believed that I was stronger, smarter, wiser, better, and more efficient than other people. I relentlessly drove my staff members to obtain organizational goals and to propel my personal power further. My self-sufficiency was my idol. Pride and arrogance were worshiped as self-confidence and self-esteem. I placed my intellect before God and could not learn or be taught in truth.

So, when my marriage began to crumble with the life I had built shaking violently, I turned to my empty silent gods of my stupid youth. And, they failed me. Jesus told the rich young man, "One thing you lack: Go your way, sell whatever you have and give to the poor, and you will have treasure in heaven; and come, take up the cross, and follow Me." It was not the "selling and giving away" that would secure eternal life, but the placing his trust in God rather than in wealth that would secure his eternal future.

The young man needed to "deny himself" by taking up the suffering and afflictions associated with being baptized in Christ. The self-denial is the killing of the old nature and becoming a new creature of holiness through the power of the Holy Spirit. Following Christ means to "leave one place" in life and move to another, one step at a time. Following Christ would mean placing Him as God first in the young man's life. That is the only way to obtain Heaven.

The wealthy man was a "good guy" just like I was a good guy. He was religious and kept the commandments of God on the surface, but lacked understanding in the deeper things of God. He had the idol of money and trusted in the power that wealth brings. He had the idol of self–sufficiency. He had the

185

idol of arrogance and self-esteem. He was strong in himself without any real need for a savior or for God.

It takes a 100% commitment to follow Christ and no less will do. You and your spouse must be committed to the eternal and not mindful of the things of this world. The things of this world are temporal and are idols. As a young man, I never counted the cost, and I succumbed to the false teachings and doctrines of Satan. This is how I became involved in the occult with its counterfeit practices. Satan easily deceived me because I had no foundation.

Without a total commitment in obedience to God, I was left to my own thoughts and devices, which brought me close to the gates of Hell. The manner in which I was running my life made it seem impossible for me to ever reach eternal thinking. If I had attempted to find God and become righteous through my own works (I tried this through spiritual practices of the occult), then it would have been impossible for me to obtain salvation. But, with God all things are possible! He revolutionized me and he can do the same for your marriage. It is possible to make the right choices, repent of sin, and give your life totally to Christ.

So, you say that your marriage is messed up and you are a chief sinner. That is good because Christ came to save chief sinners not the religious minded. He wants to set your marriage on the things of God not religion. The first step in the restoration of my marriage to Linda was to tear down the idols of self-sufficiency in my life. As the Holy Spirit guided and taught us, we were able to recognize and remove those areas in our marriage that came before God.

Embrace Correction

The reader must understand that there is no "arrival" in Christ where Satan is no longer either tempting you or allowed to "test" you according to God's sovereign will and purpose. Once, you and your spouse have committed to God, there is nothing Satan can do to you that God has not allowed. Yes, God is in control of everything. It is bad theology to entertain the notion once people come to God through Christ that all of Satan's schemes go away. No. They stay, but the power of the Holy Spirit in the believer overcomes and is victorious through Christ, who gives believers all authority over Satan, and who uses these afflictions and trials to "grow" us. To better understand the differences in demonic attacks, the following is a brief explanation of three tactics Satan uses against you and your marriage.

Temptations: Satan uses "temptations" to lure you away from what you know to be right and correct living. Once there is an "open door" and you give him permission to harass you, he comes in like a flood and carries you away into a dark place. These are the times that "you" allow Satan into your life and give him free access. When you yield to temptation or hold onto past hurts and offences, Satan will use these things against you. These are open doors. You have given him free and unlimited access to your life.

187

The sin is not in the temptation, but in the response to it. You must shut the door to evil. Imagine coming home and finding an intruder in your house stealing and destroying your property. You would call the police, and through their authority arrest the intruder and charge them with the crime of burglary. The burglar has no permission to be in your house. He is unwelcome. Now imagine the same scenario, but the burglar is your crazy drunk uncle that has both your house key and permission to enter anytime he wishes. The police and judicial system can do little for you because you have allowed the theft and destruction to occur.

Allowing Satan access to your life through yielding to temptation is no different. Ephesians 4:23, 24, and 27 state, that Christ followers need to be renewed in the spirit of their minds, putting on the new person that God created in holiness and in right standing. This is so we do not "give place to the devil."

Consequences: Oftentimes, you may be troubled in life, not by Satan, but by the consequences of your own actions and poor decisions. Although you were the one who initially brought the problems to your own door, they often give Satan an opportunity to move in and use them to his benefit and to your destruction.

A proper relationship with God and continual growth in the truth of Scripture will eliminate or minimize these times. These actions or behaviors require repentance and grace. For example, if you lived in sin by treating your spouse and children poorly, the consequences of your actions may be divorce. Subsequently, after your divorce you may repent and become a Christ follower. You may want to reconcile with your family, but as they continue to reject you, it is because of the "consequences" of your past behavior.

If someone manages money poorly and has a spending problem, then the consequences are great debt. Satan did not cause the debt, the person did, but Satan will use the guilt, shame, and pressures to work out his schemes and devices on the burdened individual. Repentance, proper Biblical financial teaching, and assistance from the Holy Spirit would be the proper course of action so that "no place is given to the devil."

Trials: Other times, you do not have an open door and have done nothing wrong, but Satan is allowed to openly attack you and test you. These are hard difficult times; God uses to "refine" your character and faith in the fire. These are the times, which the straw and stubble burn away from the brick. These are the difficult dark times, which burn the impurities from your golden faith. This is Scriptural. Satan is allowed access to you, if God permits it.

In the book of Job, Satan is given permission to test Job. In the book of Zechariah, Satan stands next to the Angel of God and accuses the high priest. In the book of Matthew, Jesus told His disciple Peter that Satan had asked permission to "sift him as wheat." Satan "hindered" the Apostle Paul when he wanted to visit the church in Thessalonica.

It is not a matter of "if," but of "when" and how often you go through trials and testing. It is not the disillusionment or the doubt that matters, but how we respond to that disillusionment and doubt. Our response is everything in warfare. This is the "pruning" of the branch, which is connected to the vine. Since you (the branch) abide in Christ (the vine), you produce the fruit of the Spirit. Often, God will prune the branch to force it to produce more fruit. This is Scriptural truth, and this is a Christ-follower reality. Sometimes God sends these afflictions to His children to keep them humble and in step with Him.

In 2Corinthians 12:7-10, the Apostle Paul writes about a "messenger of Satan" that constantly buffeted him. Paul asked Jesus to remove the "thorn in his flesh," but Christ's answer was, "My grace is sufficient for you, for My strength is made perfect in weakness." Occasionally, when trials and testing come, there can be great doubt regarding your identity in Christ. You may feel alone with your faith absolutely destroyed. You may forget that you are the branch connected to the vine. This is no easy time. It is designed to build you, to stretch you, to grow you, and to purify you in God.

You must have the Word of God ingrained in your heart and be "renewed in the spirit of your mind" (connected to the vine) so that you can reach for and grab hold of that little rope of truth when you need to pull yourself up from the belly of the pit. Listen, this is important. We are telling you that you must have the Word of God inside of you, PRIOR to your testing. Once squeezed, there has to be something that comes out. You want that something to be the Word of God. Start consuming and ingesting the Scriptures now.

Truth is important because your faith cannot anchor in the resolution of your circumstances, but has to anchor in what you know by faith to be true. When you are in the pit, it is not going to be possible to simply rebuke the devil and have him flee from you. You may find defending yourself against Satan impossible and all you can do is stand. Do everything you can do to put on the armor of God and then, stand.

Knowing the truth contained in Scripture is essential to overcoming this dark time. These dark heavy times come in all packages and can hit where you are the weakest. It could be trouble with your children, parents, boss, spouse, family, memories, attitudes, thoughts, health, or any area of your body/emotions/mind that has been damaged and is subject to attack. Often, the area of attack is the very area that God wishes to use for His glory.

A God-fearing husband or wife reminding you of the "truth" during these times of doubt and disillusionment is imperative for survival. You must be a team encouraging one another. If you and your spouse are at odds and fighting, you cannot minister to each other. Satan would love to separate you from your closest source of accountability, your spouse. Do not allow that to happen.

The following is a true story of a trial and testing that we went through a year after we had demons in our marriage bed. We both thought we were "beyond" this sort of testing and were surprised at what happened. This was a trial to build and stretch us. It was a pruning so we could produce more fruit. Remember, there is no pass or fail in this test. The test requires that you go through it – stand and believe in God's mercy. These times require you to relax in God.

During the week of March 19, 2007, Linda was directly assaulted by lies from hell. A lying spirit told her that she was going to die of a heart attack and suffocate to death (lies about death are common among many people). Linda displayed symptoms of heat in her body and tingling on her face, which are classic demonic manifestations for her. These symptoms would appear whenever an evil presence was near her.

On Sunday, March 25, 2007, before going to church, Linda told me about the demonic lies she had heard all week and how the spirit of fear was attempting to influence her. I placed my hands on her and commanded, "In the name and authority of Jesus Christ my Lord, I come against this lying spirit and bind it." I then reminded her of the importance of telling me these things when they occur so she would not suffer alone, but have me pray with her. She became slightly agitated saying, "You always get angry if I don't say anything." I immediately recognized the words as coming from a demonic influence, not from Linda, and so I put my finger up and said, "Stop, stop, stop. I reject that insecurity in the name of Jesus."

I was speaking to the lying spirit, not to Linda. It had nothing to do with her, but everything to do with Satan. It was harsh. My words and actions were abrupt and forceful because I did not want to give the lying spirit any place to talk and influence Linda's thoughts. Linda suddenly looked better and left to get ready for church. She was fine with what happened.

As soon as she left, and not a second later, I suddenly felt guilty for being harsh with her. I immediately started to doubt my actions and behaviors and questioned, "Was I operating in the Spirit or in the flesh?" Yet, I knew that my stern rebuke was at the lying spirit and not my wife. However, now I felt terrible about it. I then inquired of God. I said, "Please God, I need an answer now, not later, but now!"

God met me. He reminded me of the time when the Pharisees accused Jesus of casting out devils by the power of Satan, and how Jesus spoke to them harshly and sternly. He spoke against the demonic influenced thought process, not at the men. We read this passage of Scripture and tend to think that the Pharisees were bad men and enemies of Jesus, that there was a war going on between them. Yet, this was not the case. In Jesus' time, the Pharisees were revered leaders of the law. They were respected and had much authority. Jesus loved these men and wanted them to come to the truth and so He rebuked the lying demonically influenced speech that came from their minds and then their mouths.

This was not an attack on the individual, but on the influencing spirits. So, God reminded me that my actions were the same. God reminded me of what he already taught me about spiritual warfare, and asked, "Why would this be any different?" God reminded me of love. He urged, "Go hug Linda, tell her you love her, and explain what happened." I did this and all was well. The reader can see how the enemy works. Satan wants to confuse, cause fear and doubt. He wants to get you and your spouse to fight and separate.

While continuing to pray, God took me to another place in my thoughts. "Satan has asked to test you guys. This is why you felt disconnected all week. Had you given in and listened to your old sad rock music, you would not have believed in the authority you possess in order to come against the devil today." Because I had felt apathetic all week, it would have been easy for me to give in and resign from active spiritual warfare, but I did what I "naturally" would not do – inquire of God. This is what saved me today.

When Satan rose up, I had connection by faith, not feelings. The mind prevents us from moving forward in God. It stops us. We over think circumstances. We need to be simple. Think simple. I could hear God lament, "If only all believers had just a kernel of real faith, who really believed that the entire God of the created universe actually lived in them, they could be used in miraculous ways."

194

This is what great people in the past had, a kernel of real faith. They knew that God dwelled in them. God is not looking for great people. He has plenty of great and talented people. He is looking for usable people. Try this experiment. Have your spouse or someone else stand stiff and rigid, tensing up every muscle in their bodies. Now gently push them and you will find they easily move from place to place because their feet have to adjust and go wherever you desire. Now have the person relax their body as they stand. Gently push them and you will see that their bodies "flow" with the force and their feet stay planted.

God desires from us the same "relaxation," "flow," and "resilience." God can use you if you relax in Him, yield to Him. Likewise, in fighting arts, a skilled fighter knows that an opponent's entire body is controlled if his head can be controlled. There is a saying, "The body goes where the head goes." It does not matter how big or strong a man is, if his physical head is under the control of another then his entire body will follow. This is like spiritual warfare. If Satan can control your head (thoughts) then he can control your entire body (outcomes).

If God controls your thought processes, then He can use you for His glory. Think about a great and talented musician. For example, think about a phenomenal guitarist. The musician does not play the way he does because of the guitar. He plays the way he does because of who he is.

The guitar cannot play itself or add anything to the way it is played. The guitar is simply used by the master musician. The master chooses the guitar for its sound qualities, internal wiring, type of wood, smoothness of neck, and ease of use. The master may use a beat up old guitar because he likes the way it feels, or he may use an expensive one because he likes the way it looks. Yet, when someone else picks up the instrument, they cannot play like the master musician because it is not in the guitar, but in the player.

This is relaxing in God. Become an instrument for use and allow the master to play you. It does not matter what kind of guitar you are because it is the master who chooses and plays.

The above lesson we saw before us as we missed several opportunities for ministering to others. One was at church the night prior, when a brother was tired and feeling ill. God impressed Linda and I to say a prayer for him, but we failed to obey and move out in faith. The other opportunity was with a woman friend of ours who was experiencing great difficulties within her family. Once again, we were impressed to pray for her, but our minds got in the way.

We came up with every excuse not to pray and so we failed to do so. Our minds were hindering us. We over thought things. Reasoning instead of obeying always brings confusion. We listened to the lies, "What will they think of us? Who am I to minister to this person? They will think we are trying to be spiritual." We had to remember the usable vessel lesson.

How can God use us in mighty ways when we cannot function in small ways? We must yield to God and allow Him to play us, to use us in a unique and non-traditional way. We are the instruments and He is the player. To relax, yield, form, and flow is to be the standard mode of operation. Do not allow the mind to hinder, to over think the situation. This was a pruning so that Linda and I could produce more fruit of the Spirit.

The Burning

The first half of this story is about being pruned, the second half is definitely about being burned by fire. After Linda and I talked that Sunday morning and God showed us some things about demonic thought and speech, we went to church. We attended our regular worship service on Saturday nights and then attended the Hispanic Ministries service on Sunday mornings. Although we did not understand the Spanish language, we loved going to these services because the move of God was so strong among the people.

We liked supporting the pastor, and the ministry and were getting more and more involved with the congregation. Trying to understand the songs and the sermon was akin to trying to understand and learn the language of God – seeing through a dark glass. Yet, it was a beautiful time of worship. On this particular Sunday service, we felt the presence of God and there was an "altar call" at the end of the service with many of the congregation going up for prayer.

I (Paul) had a strong "urge" to pray for the people, and so I stood in a corner and outstretched my hands toward the people praying there. After some time elapsed, I had the "urge" to lay hands or touch the shoulders of one particular man kneeling down. I really believed God was urging me in this direction, and so I placed my hands on the back of his shoulders and began to pray in the Spirit for him. As I prayed, I felt the man's burden break. He began to cry and find release. I then slowly moved back to my chair without the man seeing me or knowing who had prayed with him.

Because I did not see any other staff members or people praying for those at the front of the church, I began to question whether I violated some sort of protocol. I could not understand the language, and so I thought maybe I did something I should not have. After the service, I inquired about the protocol regarding praying for others because I did not want to overstep boundaries.

Believe me, I understand boundaries in church because I had seen many abuses while growing up in a Pentecostal church. I was told that because the pastor knew me, it was probably all right for me to pray for the man, but normally they would not want others to get the wrong idea and think that everyone was welcome to minister and cause possible confusion. However, I was told, if the Lord was leading me to pray for someone, then I should pray. I understood this protocol completely. I left church and was fine.

On Monday, the next morning, I had these discouraging thoughts going on in my head. I could "see" these thoughts like a movie being played back for me. I was the audience watching myself in this movie. These thoughts from Hell said, "Look at yourself standing up there praying for people, you look stupid – that is not who you are. You hate people. Why would you think you could be some kind of vessel used of God? You broke protocol. You laid hands on a man without being asked, or authorized to do so. You blew it! Now the pastors will see you as you really are, an arrogant, power hungry, self-centered creep."

I began to feel so depressed and shameful. These thoughts just hounded me. The negative thoughts continued, "Before you had Christ in your life, you studied the occult, shamanism, and energy healing using unseen Chi energy." I heard, "You studied these things because you wanted power – power to heal and be recognized as a great healer. Now, it is the same thing. You are just using the Holy Spirit to gain power to heal and to be somebody special." I knew these thoughts were not of God, but I could not control them. I attempted to pray, but felt disconnected with God. The only thing I could eek out was, "Lord, show grace and mercy to me."

I knew I should be submitting and resisting, engaging in spiritual warfare, but felt so powerless although I knew deep down that I was not. Linda could sense something was wrong. She prayed. I became agitated and frustrated. I knew by faith what was truth, yet my mind was totally out of control with depression, doubt, and sadness. Can the reader see how Satan attacks?

On Sunday morning, I was filled with the Holy Spirit ministering to people and on Monday morning, I was in a deep dark cavern filled with doubt and discouragement. How did this happen? I did nothing to either open the door to the devil, or to suffer consequences for bad behavior. This was an attack.

This was war and my enemy was beating me up. On Tuesday, March 25, 2007, I did not feel right. Something was very wrong. I had to attend a business meeting and so I drove an hour alone with my negative thoughts and depression. I felt worthless. As I drove, my mind focused on the negative. I could not break it. I tuned the radio to a Christian station to hear God's Word, but I did not get anything from it. I could not concentrate on the message.

The preacher on the radio was annoying me (that is a good indicator that one is under demonic attack when the Word of God is annoying). I could not pray. I could only ask God for mercy – that is all I could say. It felt so dark. Suddenly, I started to feel ill. I was coughing and my entire body ached. The demonic attack "felt" just like the demonic attacks I used to have in the past before I totally submitted to God's authority. Yet, I knew it was different. It felt the same, but it was not the same. It seemed to me that the demonic attack was mimicking the original. It was not real.

However, I gave into the sadness and began to listen to one of my old rock and roll compilations. These songs made me sad and I gave into the depression. I was really messed up now. (Afterward, I removed and destroyed the rock and roll CD from my car so I would never give place to the devil again in that area).

By the time I arrived to the meeting, I was physically ill, mentally fogged, emotionally wrecked, and spiritually alone. This was an incredible experience for me. However, something inside of me said, "Paul, this is going to pass soon – it is testing you. There is nothing you can do but go with the flow." Well, I was so sick and mentally deranged that I did just that – I relaxed and let it go - knowing that I would be fine in the end. Inside, I knew that it was impossible for me to go back to the dark side. Impossible – because of God's Spirit in me.

Although this attack felt similar to past demonic oppressions, I knew within my spirit that it was different. The impression I got about this attack was that it was similar to a memory. I could have a memory about being 21 years old, but it was impossible for me to ever be that age again. Linda, who had been praying for me was led of God to send me a text message. She reiterated what I had told her last Sunday when I was strong in God. I had said to her, "Linda, when I am attacked this week, remind me of what God told me about us. Remind me that God said the devil wants to test you guys."

So, Linda reminded me of what God had revealed. Linda then wrote, "When Satan asked to sift Peter like wheat, Jesus told him that He would pray for him, that he would not lose faith. When Peter returned from the sifting he would strengthen others." Wow! This message ministered to me. It gave me much hope and assurance that my God was still in control. It was such a comfort to know that Jesus was praying for me at the time.

Linda's message to me was the breaking point in my depression. This is why it is vitally important that both husband and wife are walking in the Spirit and ready for spiritual warfare. Linda sent me a "word" and, that word grew in me and gave me hope and faith. Your spouse is your first line of defense and support in the battle for your marriage. Had Linda not been obedient to the voice of God, I would have continued in my funk and not been released.

It was just as much a lesson in obedience for her as it was for me. Prior to walking into the business meeting, I told God, "I certainly hope you don't send anyone my way that needs help because I am too messed up to minister in any way." I told God, "If you send someone to me in need, I am not going to respond because I cannot do it right now." I felt so bad, sick, and fuzzy that I knew everyone would see it all over my face. Yet, when I walked in, people commented on how happy I looked. Over again they made remarks about my constant smile. Yet, inside I felt horrible.

What was going on? It seemed that this attack was different in that it did not change my appearance, and I was still emitting the joy of Christ although inside I felt very bad. People had no idea what was happening to me internally. They only saw the outside. I was not pretending, I felt horrible and too week to pretend. They saw what God wanted them to see. Suddenly, I found myself in conversation with a co-worker. I told him I was trying to learn Spanish and then found myself talking to him about our church's Hispanic Ministries and how good it was to be with God's people there. Then as if I had no control over my body, I blessed him in Spanish. I said, "Dios Ti Bendiga." This blessing blew him away and his surprise was evident on his face.

However, I was more surprised because blessing someone was the last thing I wanted to do. I felt so sick and depressed. How could blessing come from my lips? I had the thought, "This is God, not the vessel. It is only by God." In my extreme weakness, God was strong. I could do nothing, yet things were happening because of the Master Potter and not the pot. Understand that people want prosperity, joy, peace, and spiritual gifts. God wants broken vessels – usable vessels.

I had always thought in the past that one had to "be on" in order to minister to others, but not so. God can use a vessel at anytime if the vessel is yielding, no matter what condition it is in. After the meeting, I drove home and no longer had any desire to listen to my sad rock and roll music. I tuned the radio to a Christian station and listened to a sermon on broken vessels. I heard the preacher say, "It was when the woman broke the vessel at Jesus' feet that the fragrance then filled the entire house." This ministered to Jesus.

God wants broken vessels and I was certainly one. By the time I arrived home, the depression and fog had lifted and I was all right. It was one of the strangest experiences. It was not something I could fix or bind or demand release, but something I just had to experience and endure. God showed His love and might in many ways that day. It was a day of burning. The straw and stubble burned from the brick, and the precious metal was refined with its dross heated in the fire of God.

Chapter 11: Tactics of Your Enemy

Prepare For Battle

Ephesians 6:10-20 proclaims, "Put on all the armor that God supplies. In this way you can take a stand against the devil's strategies" (GWT). This is war! Your marriage, family, and lives are at stake. No question about it, you had better learn to fight and you had better learn to tap into the authority, weapons, and resources God has provided for you through His Son, Jesus Christ. You must understand that Christ's work is done. He is not going chase the devil away from you so you can live a nice little happy life without challenges and problems.

God wants to refine you, to burn the chaff, to renew your heart and mind, and to circumcise your very soul. This accomplished through "growth" in Christ. You get peace, joy, and a sound mind, which far exceeds our superficial "happiness." This state does not just "come" to a person. One is broken, renewed in mind, and transformed in character. The Spirit of God works in us, teaching us all things. The Holy Spirit teaches us the art of war against our spiritual enemies, which exist to destroy us.

Because Christ has completed His work on the cross and through the resurrection, the devil is defeated. We must exercise our authority in Christ to resist Satan's temptations and strongholds. We start by making choices. Two choices are available – live for God or live against God. This is the beginning of our training in a Martial Marriage.

We fight against unseen enemies and must train in the unseen realm. Our art is one of violence, of pulling down strongholds, of casting down imaginations, of binding and of loosing. It is the violent and aggressive art of casting out, coming against, taking hold, tearing down, building up, speaking forth, reaching out, grabbing, snatching, and laying on of hands.

We hold the keys to the Kingdom of Heaven with all of its weapons and angelic resources to fight this war. Understanding how the enemy of your marriage operates is foundational to spiritual warfare and learning spiritual warfare. We fight to win. Christ came to destroy the works of our enemy and we are in Christ and He in us. We are soldiers. We are men and women full of the Holy Spirit and faith. We are warriors. Let us begin our training. Keep your focus on becoming a vicious spirit fighter, relentless and unstoppable through the power of the all mighty God.

Reality and Truth

One of the first things you must understand is that Satan is a liar, and the only truth is contained in God's Word. When Satan comes to you or your spouse with lies and falsehoods, you must rely on what the Word of God says and not the "reality" of the situation. There is a difference between "reality" and "truth."
Understanding this is essential in your battle for your marriage.

Satan rules this world and its philosophies. He creates or manipulates its "realities" also. He manipulates perceptions, facts, and realities within his kingdom. What may seem to you as a fact or a reality, it is not truth. Only God's Word is truth. Because Satan is the father of all lies (the originator of all falsehood), and there is no truth found in him, then it stands to reason the world's realities are lies also. This is why faith in God is essential and paramount. The Holy Spirit will lead you into all truth. This is why it is impossible to please God without faith. You must have faith in God's truth and not in Satan's realities.

When the world tells your husband, "It is natural for a man to have 700 sexual thoughts a day as long as it does not harm anyone," then it is time to reveal to him what the Word of God says about holiness, purity of thought, and about lusting in the mind. The Scriptures call us to be like Christ. Did God make flesh to think 700 sexual thoughts per day? No! Do you see the difference between Satan's reality and God's truth?

When the television directs your wife to overspend, to shop until she drops, and collect 365 pairs of shoes, you need to tell her about God's truth. Is she called to be in debt and in bondage? Is she called to be greedy and temporal minded? What does God say about contentment and about His provision? Every time the world or Satan whispers a "reality" in your ear, it must be compared to the Word of God for truth.

However, if your marriage is not inclined to commune with God and study His precepts, then you will have no measuring rod to differentiate between a lie and a truth and will succumb to Satan's deceit. How can you have faith in God's Word if you do not know what the Word says?

So, the choice must be made to commune with God. The choice must be made to "choose" God over your own natural desires. The choice must be made to serve, commit to, and submit under God. It is that simple. The following chapters will assist you in making the correct choice to serve God and will enlighten you to the tactics and strategies of Satan to destroy your marriage. Satan does not want you to gain close fellowship with God, so that he can use his deception to separate you and your spouse.

Blessings and Curses

There are only two ways or paths to conduct your life. We tend to make the choice difficult and complicated because of our human sinful nature. But, in all spiritual truth, the choice is simple. Even with this simple choice – choosing is not so simple for us because of our nature. We must have the mercy and grace of God to enable us to move forward in putting on the character of Christ - putting on Christ like an overcoat.

Sometimes we need help getting our arms through the coat sleeves and assistance getting the collar and buttons aligned, and that is why Jesus gave us His Holy Spirit. Yet, we must make the choice to flee from all appearance of evil. We must make the choice to live for God or live for Satan. There is no gray area. It is black and white. Quit sinning, repent, obey, and start living in holiness, being set apart for God. That is the only choice. If you are serious about a renewed marriage, then you must follow the Word of God.

I (Paul) made so many wrong choices leading up to my affair. There were many "red flags" that I simply chose to ignore. There were also numerous warning signs in our marriage in general that both Linda and I refused to face. Not making a decision for good is making a decision for bad. Months after being rescued and redeemed, I still had much confusion and demonic influence over my thoughts. This was caused in part by my inability and unwillingness to totally give up every idol, stronghold, and soul-tie related to the other woman.

My thoughts would waver. At times, I knew that I wanted to stay with Linda and renounce my relationship with the other woman, and then, other times would find me longing for another life with Riana. I was very confused and my mind was so unstable that I felt like I was slipping into a dark insane world with no return. I could not trust myself.

The problem was that I would not make the right choice to serve God. I had a simple choice. I had to commit to loving, obeying, and serving God. I had to commit to releasing my "idols" of lust and sin, and until I made the decision to live earnestly for God, I was tormented. Satan had a stronghold in my life. Satan had me as a prisoner of war – an ineffectual Christian. However, I allowed him to do it to me. I a-l-l-o-w-e-d it! Absolute commitment to God and His ways are the only means to break out of Satan's prison. By continually living in sin, I had cursed myself. God could not bless me in this state.

There is a fascinating story contained in the book of Numbers chapters 22-25, about blessings and curses. The story illustrates how no one can curse you when God has blessed and protected you. When you remove yourself from God through disobedience and sin, then you bring curses upon yourself and God will not shield you from the consequences of your actions.

One of the actions that bring curses is "idolatry." Anytime you move away from worshipping God and move toward adoring and worshiping a false god, curses on your life will follow. You must be careful that you place nothing before the Lord. The story in Numbers starts with the young nation of Israel traveling and camping in the plains of the nation of Moab. The Moabite king was terrified of what he saw because he knew that the many people of Israel would soon take over his country. The king sent for a prophet named Balaam to come and "curse" the Israelites so the king would have a fighting chance against them.

Three times the prophet attempted to curse the Israelites, but could not because God had already blessed them. Every time the prophet Balaam attempted to curse the people, God would speak forth a blessing from his lips. What God had blessed, no person could curse. God had protected His people from every evil because they were His people and He was their God.

All men were powerless to do anything against the will of the Lord. But, in chapter 25, we read that while the Israelites were camped, some of the men defiled themselves with Moabite women. They had sex with the strange women who taught them the ways of idol worship. The New Living Translation reads, "These women invited them to attend sacrifices to their gods, and soon the Israelites were feasting with them and worshipping the gods of Moab."

God's anger burned against the Israelites because of their actions and disobedience. God told Moses to kill everyone involved in this idol worship, and 24,000 people died of a plague before God relented. Understand that in chapters 22-24, God had blessed His people and no one could curse them. Now in chapter 25, the people place themselves under a curse (a plague that killed 24,000 people) because of their sin against God.

This story parallels what happens to Christians today. You may be saved and under God's blessings and no curse can be pronounced against you. However, if you move away from God and enter into a life of continual sin and practiced disobedience, then you bring a curse upon yourself. Only repentance and the destruction of sin in your life can bring God's blessings and protection again. Satan used the temptation of the Moabite women to lead the Israelite men into sin, but Satan did not "make" them sin. They desired the lust of their carnal nature, willingly went the way of darkness into his prison and captivity, and paid the price (consequences) for their sins.

Understand that your enemy will place temptations in front of you and your spouse – do not yield to them, but resist it through the power of Christ. This is Satan's first line of attack, temptation. If he can get you to "bite," then he has won the battle. Understanding your enemy is knowing that he does not want you, your spouse (your marriage) to choose God over him, and he will stop at nothing to entice you and your spouse away from the Lord.

Likewise, you may have issues of sin and disobedience in your marriage, which prevent you from being blessed, and instead, has placed a curse on your family. It is imperative then, to invite Christ to be Lord and Master over your marriage.

Avoiding Sin

You and your spouse must learn to avoid certain behaviors and attitudes in order to be free from the enemy's snares. Understanding and recognizing Satan's traps can save you from being entangled in them. Realize behaviors and attitudes bring either a blessing or a curse on our lives. Identify modern day idols, gods, non-gods, and demons of worship. Make a choice between good and evil, and life and death.

The commandment that God requires of us is simple. The choice between life and death, good or evil is simple. You cannot have a divided mind. The simple choice is between receiving a blessing or a curse in our lives. To live life abundantly, you must love God, walk in His ways by keeping His commandments. To receive death, you must turn away from God, refuse to listen to Him, and worship other gods.

Other gods? You may say, "We don't have any graven images or statues of idols anymore." Who are the other gods that one would go serve and worship, and bring a curse on their lives? Deuteronomy 31:16-18 (NKJV) reads, "They provoked Him to jealousy with foreign gods; with abominations they provoked Him to anger. They sacrificed to demons, not to God, to gods they did not know, to new gods, new arrivals that your fathers did not fear."

Sacrifice to demons? That is a frightening statement. No one who claims to be a Christian would ever think they sacrifice to demons or to unknown gods. What are these "new gods" or newly arrived idols that we can serve? Colossians 3:1-8 (ASV) tells us what these "new gods" are. "If then ye were raised together with Christ, seek the things that are above, where Christ is, seated on the right hand of God. Set your mind on the things that are above, not on the things that are upon the earth."

Clearly, we should not obsess over the world and its philosophies of greed and perversion. By seeking heavenly spiritual things, we cross the line that says, "I am on God's side and I renounce all other gods." Remember, it is a choice. Put to death fornication, uncleanness, passion, evil desire, and covetousness, that is idolatry. For in here are the new gods, demons, and newly arrived gods.

When one is subject to these demonic influences, they serve and worship other gods! The choice is simple, God or demons. Put away anger, wrath, malice, railing, and shameful talk (Colossians 3:1-8). You see, every time you make a choice to do and think such things, you make the choice to not love your God and obey His commandments. You make the choice to turn away from God, refuse to listen to Him, and serve demons. It is that simple. If you have a divided mind, it is because you have not made a choice to be on God's side of the line. So, how do we live? How are we supposed to turn from sin and idolatry?

1John 3:4-8 (The Message) outlines how we should pursue life. "All who indulge in a sinful life are dangerously lawless, for sin is a major disruption of God's order. Surely, you know that Christ showed up in order to get rid of sin. There is no sin in him, and sin is not part of his program. No one who lives deeply in Christ makes a practice of sin. None of those who do practice sin has taken a good look at Christ. They have him all backwards. So, my dear children do not let anyone divert you from the truth. It is the person who acts right who is right, just as we see it lived out in our righteous Messiah. Those who make a practice of sin are straight from the devil, the pioneer in the practice of sin. The Son of God entered the scene to abolish the devil's ways."

One of the best defenses against the enemy of your marriage is to choose to live for God. You and your spouse must make this choice. A marriage will not fall to Satan, if both husband and wife are committed to God and quit any type of "practiced sin" in their lives. The number one tactic of your enemy is to get you to worship anything but God.

Satan Makes War

We Christians are up against a mighty formidable opponent that will tear us apart and easily destroy us if we are not totally committed to God through His Son, Jesus Christ. This is the truth. Satan is serious and dangerous. He has no remorse, no conscience, and no good or neutral intention. He is set on coming into your life and marriage and kicking you right in the face and strangling you to death. If you have committed to Christ's way of life, Satan will constantly attempt to rip you off, harass, torment, deceive, destroy, strangle, kick, punch, grab, bite, gouge, and eat you alive. It is only by the power of God through Christ that we can resist Satan. When we gain true knowledge of our authority in Christ, it is then that we can actually counter -attack his onslaught.

Following Christ is a commitment and takes picking up your cross and following Him. At first, you will only be able to resist, then when you gain more spiritual power from God, you will be able to rebel against Satan's house, tearing down strongholds and releasing others from Satan's prison and bondage. This is war. This is serious. As soon as you asked Christ into your heart, you became a warrior. Like it or not, it is all about the spiritual side. God is spirit and the war we fight is spiritual.

If you do not wish to fight Satan and only want God's blessings, we wish you luck because you and your marriage will be ineffectual at best and, utterly destroyed at worse. Unlike humans, God takes vows seriously. You made a vow to God and entered into a covenant relationship with Him when you received His salvation. To think that you can slide through a Christian life expecting only blessings and no trouble is ignorant. God will use His Spirit to quicken you, to move you, to make you get up and run toward Him. You can go the easy way or the hard way, but God takes your vow seriously and you belong to Him.

Remember, Satan absolutely hates you and your marriage. You are a human being created in the image of God and he hates God. When Satan looks at you, he sees God's creation and he wants to destroy that work of God. If you ever think Satan is your friend, you will die. If you ever think he is neutral because you feel no harassment in your life, then he already has you in his deceptive grip and you do not even know it. When God carried out His redemptive plan for humankind through the death, resurrection, and ascension of His Son Jesus, Satan was defeated. Not understanding this gives him legal right to deceive you in many ways.

In the beginning, he deceived the first man and woman. It is ironic that Satan's first recorded destruction was a marriage. The serpent was clever. Notice that Satan spoke and asked a question. He asked a simple question to engage the human in conversation that would ultimately lead to deception.

Do not listen to Satan's questions. He will ask questions about your marriage, your life, your church, your job, your sexuality, your finances, your confidence, your salvation, and other endless chatter. You must not answer him, but seek and inquire of God through prayer and the Scriptures. Remember, Satan twists the truth, lies, and deceives. His reality is not God's truth.

Never engage in conversation with Satan. The only thing you need to say to him is, "In the name (authority) of Jesus, I command you to get away from me!" When the human allowed Satan to converse with her, he was able to easily deceive her with lies because he has been lying since the beginning of time and is an expert in espionage.

Look out for the hook. One of the key elements in demonic lies is the hook of having it the "easy way." You must understand, Satan usually will not tell you to do something that takes any kind of spiritual effort (like crucifying the flesh and striving for holiness). He likes to give humans an easy way out. For example, witchcraft is a counterfeit, easy way out for gaining God's wisdom, and fortune telling is a counterfeit, easy way out opposed to having God's prophetic gift. Eve saw that the forbidden fruit looked good to eat. She realized what she would gain from eating it, wisdom and knowledge. Therefore, she took and ate the fruit, giving some to Adam.

If Satan could deceive Eve, he certainly can deceive you. The Apostle Paul wrote in 2Corinthians 11:3-4, that he was afraid because exactly as the serpent seduced Eve with his smooth talk, the church was being lured away from the simple purity of their love for Jesus.

Satan is very adept at disguise and deception. One of Satan's tricks on humans is to counterfeit God's power, but he is limited and cannot prevail if one is grounded in Christ and His Word. However, if one is not grounded, and leaves a little room of doubt for Satan to come in, then they can be taken captive. Deception will overcome even "those who ought to know better."

Fake Messiahs and lying preachers are going to pop up everywhere. Their impressive credentials and dazzling performances will pull the wool over the eyes of even those who ought to know better (Matthew 24:24, TMSG). This is why it is so important to test and discern the spirits to see if they are from God. You can test through prayer, through the Holy Spirit, and through God's Scriptures. It is imperative that you and your marriage are in right standing with God, so the enemy will not be able to easily deceive you and your family.

Power, signs, and miracles are so deceptive that many people fall prey to his lure becoming imprisoned in darkness. Satan will transform into an angel of light in order to deceive humans. Do not think for one minute that Satan only comes as a big scary monster. He is much more sly than that. He is deceptive, will impersonate an angel of light, a prophet of God, or servant of Christ. "Also, I said it once; I'll say it again: If anyone, regardless of reputation or credentials, preaches something other than what you received originally, let him be cursed" (Galatians 1:9, TMSG). We cannot stress enough these truths. Satan is a masterful deceiver and he absolutely hates you and your marriage. Because he hates you and your marriage, he wants to destroy you and prevent you from living effectively for God.

Jesus speaks of the devil in John 8:43, 44, as he chastises the religious leaders of His time. "Why can't you understand one word I say? Here is why: You cannot handle it. You are from your father, the devil, and all you want to do is please him. He was a killer from the very start. He could not stand the truth because there was not a shred of truth in him. When the liar speaks, he makes it up out of his lying nature and fills the world with lies."

Another incident of Satan using mixed error with truth to deceive and attempting to get someone to make a wrong choice is found in Matthew 4:3-11. The temptation of Christ contains Satan actually quoting Scripture to Jesus! The New Testament in Modern Speech translates the verses as, "So the Tempter came and said, 'If you are the Son of God, command these stones to turn into loaves.' 'It is written,' replied Jesus,

'It is not on bread alone that a man shall live, but on whatsoever God shall appoint.'" Notice that Jesus resists Satan through God's Word and truth.

"Then the devil took Him to the Holy City and caused Him to stand on the roof of the Temple, and said, 'If you are God's Son, throw yourself down; for it is written, 'To His angels He will give orders concerning thee, and on their hands they shall bear thee up, lest at any moment thou should strike thy foot against a stone.'" Notice here that Satan is quoting Scripture, Psalms 91:11, 12, to Jesus! Every bit of that quote is true.

So why did not Jesus fall for this Satanic "truth?" Because the quoted Scripture was taken out of the contextual meaning of the entire passage, and Satan was able to subtly twist the "truth" to attempt to get Jesus to test God's mercy. Read Psalm 91, and see that the entire passage discusses the safety of abiding in the presence of God, which verses 11 and 12 are part of the promises of security when one "dwells" with God. This passage does not list God's promises of safety and deliverance from evil, so that the reader could "test" these things to see if they are true. The safety and deliverance promises are the direct result of "abiding" under the shelter and authority of God.

Do you see the difference? Satan will quote truth. However, it will be either mingled with wrong thinking (a lie) or it may be taken out of context. Christians must not take a single verse out of context and make it work for their own purpose. We must read the entire passage, understand what the writer was conveying, and allow the Holy Spirit to reveal the truths in Scripture. The 'spirit" behind Psalm 91, is not to endorse the reader to run around like a dare-devil stunt person, placing themselves in various dangerous situations to see if God promises will really protect them from their own stupidity. Rather, the spirit behind this Scripture was to emphasize that the reader must have a proper relationship with God. "Again it is written," replied Jesus, "Thou shall not put the Lord thy God to the proof."

Once again, Jesus fights Satan's intrusion with the proper use of Scripture. It is absolutely imperative that Christians read, study, and "ingest" the Scriptures so they can be readily employed during the time of Satan's tempting, intrusion, and/or manifestation in their marriage and life. Notice this fact. Jesus knew Psalm 91 well. It is obvious by Jesus' reply to Satan that Jesus absolutely "knew" and had "faith" in God's promises of safety. Because of Jesus' "faith" in the truth, it was an incredibly ridiculous request from Satan to suggest to Jesus that He then "test" God to see if those promises were true.

Then the devil took Him to the top of an exceedingly lofty mountain, from which he caused Him to see all the kingdoms of the world and their splendor, and said to Him, "All this I will give you, if you will kneel down and do me homage." You can see here that Jesus did not engage Satan in an argument over who had more authority on earth. Soon, Jesus' death, resurrection and ascension to the right hand of the Father would defeat Satan and capture his rule and dominion.

Jesus once again, relied on His faith and knowledge of God's truth to rebuke and resist Satan's lies and harassment. "Leave Satan!" Jesus replied, "For it is written, 'To the Lord thy God thou shall do homage, and to Him alone shall thou render worship.'" Then the devil left Him, and angels at once came and ministered to Him.

We Have Authority

Never let your guard down. However, the good news is that we do not have to live our lives in torment, but can have victory. To do this, we must know and have "faith" in the authority of Jesus Christ over the demonic spirit world and have knowledge and faith that He delegated this authority to us as Christians! But, how do we recognize issues as demonic attacks and influence rather than simply being life's problems? Following are some of Satan's strategies to keep your marriage in the land of bondage and darkness.

Exodus 1:7-22, records a pattern for Satan's "strategies" on God's children. Then in Exodus 5:6-14, the "tactics" used within the strategies are listed. Finally, we will examine the "responses" listed in Exodus 5:19-23. These verses in Exodus are a "type" of spiritual warfare. I realize they are telling a historical account regarding the nation of Israel's deliverance from Egypt, but the Scriptures are alive and often God will show you other spiritual truths in them. This is one of those occasions.

To see Satan's strategies in the behavior of the King of Egypt is spiritually sound because, the spirit that was operating in him was the spirit of this world and not the Spirit of God. People who have the spirit of Satan operating in their lives will produce the same strategies and tactics that Satan himself produces. People having the Spirit of God operating in their lives will have the fruit of the Spirit. The verses tell us how Satan oppresses us and why he desires to keep our spiritual growth down. We learn a lot about the reasons why we are afflicted or oppressed. We also can see that we grow and multiply when under pressure. The story picks up after the Israelites came to Egypt under the leadership of Joseph who had favor with the King of Egypt.

However, after Joseph died and a new King ruled over Egypt, the situation changed for the Israelites. The Egyptians began to fear the Israelites and so oppressed them. Exodus 1:7 (NKJV) reads, "But the children of Israel were fruitful and increased abundantly, multiplied and grew exceedingly mighty; and the land was filled with them." As God's children under the new covenant with Christ, we are multiplied, and our power and authority in Christ far exceeds that of our enemy Satan. It is not by our power, but by the authority and power of Christ Jesus that we destroy the works of Satan. Acts 26:18 (NKJV) demands us, "To open their eyes, in order to turn them from darkness to light, and from the power of Satan to God, that they may receive forgiveness of sins and an inheritance among those who are sanctified by faith in Me." As we grow and multiply, we continue to occupy Satan's territory, this world and its system, and he does not like that fact.

Now there arose a new king over Egypt, who did not know Joseph (v.8). This king is a "type" of Satan. This king does not honor the children of God, but is afraid of them because they are mighty and are capable of going to war against him. He wants to keep them as slaves in his land so they can work, serve, and build for him. He said to his people, "Look, the people of the children of Israel are more and mightier than we." Satan says to his demonic forces, "Hey, these Christ-followers, these Spirit-filled believers in God, these people of faith that trust in God almighty are more powerful than us. They operate under the same authority of Jesus because He gave them all authority over us." Luke 10:19 assures, "Behold, I give you the authority to trample on serpents and scorpions, and over all the power of the enemy, and nothing shall by any means hurt you." Satan continues, "We do not want them to realize their standing in God, nor to realize, understand, and use their God given authority over us."

Now the King of Egypt said, "Come, let us deal shrewdly with them, lest they multiply, and it happen, in the event of war, that they also join our enemies and fight against us, and so go up out of the land (v.10)." The Hebrew Word shrewdly in the New King James Version is translated as "wisely" in the King James Version of the Bible. The Word is "chakham," which means to be prudent, cunning, clever, and to think of oneself as wise.

Now Satan continues his speech to his forces, "All demons and evil spirits, listen, we have to be cunning and deceitful when dealing with these Christ-followers. We have to keep them in blindness, darkness, deceit, and lies. If we do not deceive them, then they could possibly realize their standing in Christ and go to war against us! The Christ-followers might join others of like mind and join forces against us. If they go to war against us, we will lose because through Jesus Christ, they are more powerful. We cannot allow them to leave this land of oppression, sin, darkness, futility, and deceit."

This is the first strategy. Satan uses cunning shrewdness to deceive you and your spouse just as the King of Egypt did to the ancient Jews. The king commanded that they set taskmasters over the Jews. Currently, Satan does the same thing to Christians. He sets his demonic forces as taskmasters against us. They use humans, circumstances, and demonic spirits, to hassle, buffet, harass, agitate, depress, oppress, and destroy us.

This is the second strategy. Satan wants you and your spouse under his taskmasters. The reason is to afflict us with their burdens just as the ancient Israelites were burdened under Egypt. Satan uses the same strategies today as he did then – afflict the Christians with burdens and tasks, so that they cannot even think about deliverance or escape.

This is the third strategy. Satan wants to keep you and your spouse burdened and afflicted. "And they built for

Pharaoh supply cities, Pithom and Raamses," (V. 11). Supply cities refer to storehouses of treasure, a collection, and to gather. The devil wants to keep you and your spouse preoccupied with things, activities, and burdens of life and worldly possessions. He does this by tasking you to build up "supplies" of worldly wealth, anger, depression, pride, lack of forgiveness, and other demonic influences. The supplies that Satan has the Christian store up for him are for his use.

The arrogance, hate, and illnesses are for Satan's use against you and others. You think it is your money, your career, your success, your anger or hate, but it all belongs to the devil, if you have not submitted totally to God through Christ Jesus. Eventually, Satan will destroy everything.

This is the fourth strategy. Satan desires to keep you and your spouse running around collecting treasures on earth, thinking worldly rather than walking in the Spirit. "But the more they afflicted them, the more they multiplied and grew. And they were in dread of the children of Israel," (V. 12). But, here is the good news. The more Satan afflicts Christ's disciples, the more God "grows" his children. The more God's children are afflicted by the devil, the stronger God becomes in us because His strength is shown in our weakness. The stronger God becomes in his children's lives, the more Satan is afraid of the destruction that is soon to come.

These children will go to war and they will prevail. They cannot lose. Satan is in "fear" of Christ-followers and is repulsed by them. The kingdom of darkness "dreads" true Christians. Did you realize that your Godly marriage could cause such a violent reaction? "So the Egyptians made the children of Israel serve with rigor. They made their lives bitter with hard bondage— in mortar, in brick, and in all manner of service in the field. All their service in which they made them serve was with rigor," (V. 13,14).

Satan will continue his assaults on your marriage. He attempts to keep you and your spouse in hard bondage, making your life bitter. He continually attempts to tempt you away from the truth and deceive you into believing false doctrine.

He is a liar and the father of all lies. He will tell you, "You are bad, stupid, ugly, fat, skinny, a cheater, a liar, sick, dying, and confused." Satan wants you to be serving his interests with rigor. He does not want you to be free in the knowledge of who you really are in Christ Jesus – a son of God and if a son, a joint heir. So, how did God deliver Israel? The same way He delivered us, through a deliverer or savior. In Exodus, God used Moses to deliver His people. Now, God has delivered us through the crucifixion, resurrection, and exaltation of His Son, Jesus Christ. So, how should we live? We live in Jesus.

Recognize Tactics

Now we will explore the tactics Satan uses within the above strategies. Remember the four strategies are:

1. Shrewdness

2. Taskmasters

227

3. Burdens

4. Storehouses

Exodus 5:6-14 (NKJV), outlines what happens spiritually when people say, "Let us go and sacrifice to God." The kingdom of darkness will not sit idly by and allow your marriage to go to God without a struggle. Following are some of the "tactics" used within the above strategies to keep your marriage in the land of bondage. Pharaoh commanded the taskmasters, "You shall no longer give the people straw to make brick as before. Let them go and gather straw for themselves. You shall lay on them the quota of bricks, which they made before. You shall not reduce it. For they are idle; therefore they cry out, saying, 'Let us go and sacrifice to our God.' Let more work be laid on the men, that they may labor in it, and let them not regard false Words."

When you and your spouse agree to go sacrifice to the Lord, the tactic of demons is to lay more and more burdens on your marriage. The tactic is designed to discourage you from leaving Egypt. The desired result of this tactic is giving up and falling down under the increased pressure. This tactic falls within the strategy discussed in Exodus 1:11, of assigning taskmasters with burdens.

This is the first tactic. Satan will step it up. He will increase the burdens and afflictions in order to discourage you from thinking about God. And the taskmasters of the people and their officers went out and spoke to the people, saying, "Thus says Pharaoh: 'I will not give you straw. Go, get yourselves straw where you can find it; yet none of your work will be reduced.'" If you and/or your spouse are running around in life collecting worthless material things, then you have fallen for this tactic. If you are collecting hurts, anger, frustration, agitation, resentment, and ungodly habits, then this tactic has worked. It is designed to keep your mind away from God because of all the collecting and storing of worthless (valueless for your use, but valuable for Satan's use) treasure. The next tactic falls within the strategy outlined in Exodus 1:12, working for Satan's supply cities.

This is the second tactic. Your enemy is engaging you in worldly affairs, chasing and building worthless things. Israel's taskmasters forced them to hurry saying, "Fulfill your work, your daily quota, as when there was straw." They were rushing around. Hurried. No time. Must go. Taskmasters will force you to hurry, giving you no time for the things of God. Yet, God has to have priority in your marriage. He demands the first fruits of your labor and your time. Placing God in any other position opens the door for the taskmasters to enter into your marriage.

This is the third tactic, which falls within the strategy of Exodus 1:13. It is designed to keep your marriage burdened and serving the kingdom of darkness with "rigor." The officers of the children of Israel, whom Pharaoh's taskmasters had set over them, were beaten and were asked, "Why have you not fulfilled your task in making brick both yesterday and today, as before?" The end-result of the strategies and tactics of your enemy is to beat you down. Satan will cause the burdens of life, the intense collecting, the increased problems, the haste, and the hurry to beat you into the ground.

This last tactic is in line with the strategy written in Exodus 1:14, which states that life will be bitter with hard bondage. This is the fourth tactic. It is the result of the above strategies and tactics. It is designed to destroy your marriage. So, what was Israel's response to all of this harassment? Exodus 5:19-23 (NKJV) categorizes the responses and they were not initially good.

However, we need to learn from them so we do not respond the same. The officers of the children of Israel saw that they were in trouble after it was said, "You shall not reduce any bricks from your daily quota." First, they "saw" with their natural eyes. They "saw" the trouble all around them. They looked with natural eyes and saw what was temporal rather than eternal. Then, as they came out from Pharaoh, they met Moses and Aaron who stood there to meet them. They said to them, "Let the LORD look on you and judge, because you have made us abhorrent in the sight of Pharaoh and in the sight of his servants, to put a sword in their hand to kill us."

After seeing with the natural eyes, they "spoke" with natural lips. They actually added despair to their situation by saying that Pharaoh was going to kill them.

Death was never discussed in the previous chapters. They added it. This is called using the "imagination," and imaginations are evil things from the heart. Moses returned to the LORD and said, "Lord, why have You brought trouble on this people? Why is it You have sent me? For since I came to Pharaoh to speak in Your name, he has done evil to this people; neither have You delivered Your people at all." Moses was "grown" in God to become a great and godly leader, but at this stage of his development, he doubted.

He asks God, "Lord, why have you sent me?" You can sense the doubt, fear, and discouragement all due to seeing, speaking, and hearing in the natural. He continued the lament, "Neither have you delivered your people at all." Moses forgot all of the promises God gave him back in Chapter 3:18-22. It is truly impossible to please God without faith. So, the Exodus principle is applying eternal faith to your temporal circumstances.

Our proper response is:

1. Do not look, speak, and hear in the natural, but have faith in God.

2. Do not lose heart, but be strong and courageous in God.

3. Do not forget the promises of God.

Satan's Kryptonite

Do you remember the comic book hero, Superman? There have been movies and television programs based on this fictitious comic strip superhero. Superman was from another planet, which was destroyed, and he was sent to earth as a baby to do good and right things. On earth, this child had super powers of strength, x-ray vision, speed, and a host of other extraordinary talents and abilities. It seemed that Superman was invincible.

However, there was one substance that made him weak and could cause death. This substance was called Kryptonite, named after Superman's original planet Krypton. The very thing that gave him superpowers (coming from the planet Krypton) was the very thing that made him weak (pieces of his planet on earth). The same weapons used to defeat Satan are the same weapons he wishes to reverse and use on your marriage.

Satan wishes to bring a child of God, their spouse and children to a place in life for destruction or ineffectiveness in their Christian witness. These pieces of "Kryptonite" will weaken you and/or your marriage and will cause you to be bound to Satan's lies and darkness. You can be sure, he will throw these at you continually, but you can resist their effects through proper living outlined in 2Peter 1:5-19, which we will discuss after the following points.

Immorality: If Satan can get you, a Christian, to compromise your values and live in immorality, he has already won the battle against you. This immorality is not limited to sexual sin, but encompasses all moral and ethical behavior outlined in the Scriptures. Remember, it is what you do in secret that determines your character. Continued immorality will destroy your marriage.

Spiritual Ignorance: Once Satan defeats you in the area of morality, I guarantee that the studying, embracing, and living in God's Word will be the last thing you want to do. Understand that if you really live God's Word, then immorality cannot overtake you because of the conviction of wrongdoing by the Holy Spirit. Satan's first tactic is to remove you from God's Word. Only then are his lies easier to accept. It is important that both husband and wife engage the Scriptures individually and collectively. There will be no accountability to one another if there is no embracing of God's Word. Satan would love to defeat your marriage through Scriptural ignorance. It is only through the Word of God that we can know the difference between the devil's lies and truth.

Out of Control: The lack of self-control can lead to all kinds of sins. The Scriptures are clear that it is "we" who have to resist the devil, fight the fight, stand our ground, wrestle against spiritual beings, bring our thoughts into captivity, love one another, etc. We as Christians must "press" forward in our walk with God. This entails self-control. The Holy Spirit will assist, guide, remind of sin, and comfort us. However, He cannot do this if we are out of control, living in immorality and removed from the Word of God. A sure way to lose your marriage to Satan is for one or both spouses to be out of control.

Impatience: Without self-control how can you be patient? How can you wait on the Lord for answers and direction if you are out of control, living immorally, and ignoring His Word? Patient endurance of life's trials, troubles, and tribulations can only be accomplished through the power of the Holy Spirit. Once patience has developed in you, then you can be presented in perfection to God. Because you are one flesh with your spouse, you will often experience trials and troubles collectively. Understanding and having faith in God's Word is essential to withstanding these troubles in life. Patient endurance of trials and troubles will not occur if one is living a sinful and out of control lifestyle.

Ungodly Living: This is the opposite of godliness. It is impossible to have the character of Christ, if one is living in immorality, lacks self-control, ignores God's Word, and lacks patient endurance. Satan may not attempt to take you here immediately, but slowly little by little by compromising you on some or all of the above points.

Hatred for the Church: Scripture exhorts us over again to love one another. We should have patience, kindness, thoughtfulness, gentleness, and love with our brothers and sisters in the Lord. This includes displaying genuine love for your spouse, as they are partners with you in the godly inheritance. Of course, loving people in the church will be the last thing on your mind if living an out of control, immoral, Godless life with no patience or spiritual understanding.

Hate for Everyone: Having love for everyone is hard enough with the help of the Spirit. I cannot imagine trying to display godly love and concern for strangers without the indwelling of God's character in one's life. Satan will not even need to dip down to this level as hatred for your fellow man will come "naturally" living an out of control, Godless, and impatient life coupled with immoral and unethical behavior. Your hatred for the world will spill over into your marriage, causing great strife and divides. This is just what Satan wants. I believe you can see that succumbing to one or all of the above satanic tactics will rob you of living a victorious life in Christ.

The "Kryptonite" will make you weaker and weaker until you and your marriage are ineffective and useless to the mission of Christ. This is a sad state to be in because most Christians do not even realize what is happening to them spiritually. If they are in this state of bondage, it is because they have not taken the practice of the Scriptures seriously.

There is a way out and a way of prevention. It is just the opposite of what Satan wants to do in your marriage. It is Satan's Kryptonite. Doing the following will make his bondage and hold on your life and marriage weaker and weaker. Following these principles will give you victory in your life with Christ. They will make you useful for the mission of Christ. They will give you purpose.

2Peter 1:5-11 (NASB) reads, "Now for this very reason also applying all diligence, in your faith supply moral

excellence, and in your moral excellence knowledge."
Add "moral excellence" to your Christian walk. Then
add knowledge of the things of God. This is
foundational. You cannot have godliness if you do not
have moral excellence and you cannot have godliness if
you do not know what the character of godliness is.
Scriptural knowledge is essential to knowing the will
and purpose of God.

Verse six continues, "And in your knowledge, self
control, perseverance, add godliness." Understanding
the nature of God through Jesus Christ will teach about
self-control and by living a moral life. The Holy Spirit
is allowed to guide and direct you in all things. Having
built on this foundation, then you can persevere trials.
Adding godliness or the character of Christ in your life
and marriage, leads to kindness and love.

One can see that it is impossible to add the character
and nature of Christ if one is living in sin. Working
hard on the above principles will ensure a godly life.
The final mixture is love for your fellow Christians.
This is accomplished by adhering to the above
principles. It is impossible to minister to others both
inside and outside the body of Christ if one does not
have genuine Christ-centered love. It is this love for the
church and for the lost, which allows the Christian to
complete the great commission to lead others to the
saving knowledge of Christ Jesus.

Verse eight summarizes, "For if these qualities are
yours and are increasing, they render you neither
useless nor unfruitful in the true knowledge of our Lord

Jesus Christ." "If" these things are present in your life and are present in your marriage and abound, then you and your marriage will be useful and purposeful to the Kingdom of God.

"For he who lacks these qualities is blind or short-sighted, having forgot his purification from his former sins" (verse nine). This is the sorry state, which Satan would like to keep all Christians. Shortsighted and blind, the person cleansed from their sins fails to turn away from their old behaviors and attitudes, which leads them into bondage and uselessness.

Remember Satan is a counterfeiter. He has counterfeited the principles of 2Peter 1:5-11, and reversed their impact for the negative outcome of imprisoning you and your marriage. "Therefore brethren, be all the more diligent to make certain about His calling and choosing you; for as long as you practice these things, you will never stumble."

Verse 11 concludes, "For in this way the entrance into the eternal kingdom of our Lord and Savior Jesus Christ will be abundantly supplied to you." You will never stumble. God's Word is straightforward. If one is to follow these principles and actually add to their faith the above listed actions, they will have a grand entrance into the Kingdom of God! You can see why this passage is Satan's Kryptonite. It absolutely weakens his power and destroys strongholds on your life and marriage.

However, reversing the principles and doing the opposite is Kryptonite to you. Examine your life right now and see if any of these principles and "calls to action" has been reversed in your life, or in your marriage. Maybe you lack morality, still surfing pornography on the Internet, or still addicted to sexual romance novels. Maybe you and your spouse have quit reading the Scriptures individually or collectively. Are any of you out of control in your thoughts, behaviors, attitudes, and emotions?

How well do you respond to adversity? Does adversity in your life draw you closer to God, or does it destroy you? Do you lack the character of godliness or do you have animosity for the children of God? Do you want to kill your neighbor? Have you experienced road rage recently? Is anger, immorality, impatience, and sin a habitual part of your life and marriage? If any of these things are true, then repent and ask God to forgive your sins through the Lord Jesus Christ. Turn away from your sin and then begin to follow the "Peter Principles" outlined above.

Your life and marriage are useless and ineffective if this is not accomplished. Satan will continue to have free reign in your life and marriage, causing confusion, strife, stupor, discontent, and bondage. You will never be free and complete in Christ until you totally repent and turn away from all appearance of evil.

Chapter 12: Defeating Your Enemy

"No one engaged in warfare entangles himself with the affairs of this life, that he may please him who enlisted him as a soldier."-2Timothy 2:3-6

By now you know that Satan will attack you and your marriage. He will come at you and your spouse in every direction. He has been lying, deceiving, and making war on God's people for millennium and so, he is very good at it. Without the knowledge of spiritual warfare and protection of the Holy Spirit, you will be destroyed and devoured by this enemy. Let us recap.

1. Do not think for one moment that you are involved in a "fair fight." Do not think that this is a little shoving match or sport-wrestling exhibition. You and your marriage are in a fight for life! You must fight off the enemy as your very life depended on it, because it does. This is not a fight, but combat. You and your spouse are in mortal combat with this enemy. Why does Satan want to ruin your marriage?

2. Your marriage is a microcosm of the church. The Scriptures talk about the relationship between Christ and His bride-church and a husband and his bride-wife. You can attend church, be involved in ministry, sing in the choir, be on staff, and still not be accountable to anyone. One can fake it. One can fool the masses. The one who is really close to you, the one who lives with you, the one who knows you like the back of their hand is your spouse. They are the only ones who can really

hold you accountable to godly living because they are intimate with you, both emotionally and spiritually.

3. Just because you belong to a church does not mean that other members will know your sin, evil desires, lusts, secret activities, or lack of Christian living. But, your spouse will notice. They will see a change in you and they will know something is not right. This is one of the reasons why Satan wants to destroy your marriage relationship – because it removes your immediate help and strength.

Deuteronomy 25:17-19 contains a command, which God gave the Israelites. This command speaks about a race of people known as the Amalekites who continued to harass and make war with Israel. These evil warriors used sneaky tactics to kill, maim, and wound the weak and famished Israelites that lagged behind the main group while on their long journey in the wilderness. The Amalekites attacked the stragglers and the tired. These warriors had no fear of God. God commanded the Israelites to destroy this race because if their heartless attacks on His people.

The Amalekites disappeared off the face of the earth because Israel destroyed them as God commanded. There is a spiritual lesson in this Scripture. Satan attacks you and your marriage just like the Amalekites attacked Israel. Satan is sneaky, merciless, and without respect for God. During our spiritual fight, Satan and his demons had continually attacked us at all hours of the night and day. They were relentless and we were so tired. We could not sleep, and mental fatigue took over like a dark cloud. The more we struggled to survive, the more Satan engaged us in combat, trying to rip us apart. He wanted to devour us.

One day, God gave us this Scripture. We noticed the parallel right away between the Amalekite attacks on Israel and Satan's attacks on us. But, look at the end of the Scripture and you will find victory over the enemy. God stated that when His people obtained "rest" in the land, He was giving them, then, they were to kill Amalek. They were to never forget! Likewise, once God took us to the place of His rest and peace, and once, we were able to get to the "roots" of the demonic strongholds in our lives, and once we learned our authority in Christ, we were able to conduct spiritual warfare.

"Do not forget what Amalek did to you on the road after you left Egypt, how he attacked you when you were tired, barely able to put one foot in front of another, mercilessly cut off your stragglers, and had no regard for God. When God, your God, gives you rest from all the enemies that surround you in the inheritance-land, God, your God, is giving you to possess, you are to wipe the name of Amalek from off the Earth. Don't forget," (Deuteronomy 25:17-19, GWT).

How do we protect ourselves from Satan's attacks while we go about destroying his kingdom? Ephesians 6 is the definitive manual for conducting spiritual warfare. Finally, receive your power from the Lord and from His mighty strength. First, you must get your power and strength from God. You cannot do battle with Satan with human skills, talents, or intelligence because he will kill you in battle. You get power from God by "abiding" in Christ, obeying His commandments in Scripture, and loving others. You get power to combat Satan through knowing God's Word and through knowing God through prayer.

Without the proper relationship with God the Father, your combat against the kingdom of darkness is futile. Put on all the armor that God supplies. In this way, you can take a stand against the devil's strategies. All of the armor must be used, not just what you are comfortable with, or what you believe is appropriate. In this way, you can stand. You can fight and press forward in battle because everyday is a battle. Everyday is a skirmish. Everyday Satan desires to imprison you and destroy your marriage. This is not a wrestling match against a human opponent. We are wrestling with rulers, authorities, the powers who govern this world of darkness, and spiritual forces that control evil in the heavenly world. This is not a wrestling match, but is all out war!

The enemy of your marriage brings forth all the forces of the kingdom of darkness with all its power and control to annihilate your marriage. This is nothing to take lightly. For this reason, take up all the armor that God supplies. Then you will be able to take a stand during these evil days. Once you have overcome all obstacles, you will be able to stand firm.

Notice that the Scripture does not say you and your marriage will not be attacked, if you put on the armor of

God. It gives no promise of peace. It gives no assurance you will not be assaulted. What it does say is that you will be able to overcome all obstacles through the armor of God, and once that happens, you will be able to stand your ground. You will not be destroyed. So then, take your stand!

Fasten truth around your waist like a belt. Put on God's approval as your breastplate. Stand! Fight! The war is on! Hang on and buckle up because you may be going for quite a ride. The truth around your waist is contained in the knowledge of God's Word and His Scriptures. You see, because Satan is such a prolific liar it is essential that you know the truth. Only by knowing the truth will you be able to tell falsehood. Understand this; **IT IS NOT WHAT YOU FEEL, IT IS WHAT YOU KNOW!** Feelings are deceptive and come from our human emotions. One of Satan's favorite tactics is to deceive you and your spouse through emotions. You must know that you know. Remember, it is not what you feel - it is what you know!

Putting on God's righteousness or approval means knowing that you are abiding in Christ and He in you. You and your spouse must live in Christ to combat Satan. In order to cover your heart and other vital organs, you must have the covering of "right standing" with God. You must know that your relationship is right with Him.

Put on your shoes so that you are ready to spread the good news that gives peace. In the midst of your battle, you can find something to praise God for. You can thank Him for allowing the attack because you have grown in the knowledge of warfare. You can spread the good news of God's redemption to others through your trials and tribulations. Sharing your story is essential to helping others find freedom from Satan's lies and strongholds.

In addition to all these, take the Christian faith as your shield. With it you can put out all the flaming arrows of the evil one. Without faith in your weapon system, you will fail in combat. One must know and be confident in the weapons they use against their enemies. Without belief and trust in God's Word, then Satan can easily penetrate your mind and deceive you.

Once again, it is not what you feel, rather, it is what you know, what you believe, and what you trust in that will assist you in battle. Your marriage must be shielded and covered in faith that God will bring you and your spouse to victory through His Son, Jesus Christ.

Also, take salvation as your helmet, and the Word of God as the sword that the Spirit supplies to you. Once Satan can lie to you and make you believe that you can be separated from God's love and mercy, then he can begin working on your faith in salvation. Once he gets you to question your salvation, then he has you in his grasp and can torment your marriage over again. Without full confidence in your salvation through Christ, how can you resist the other numerous lies from the enemy? How can you and your spouse be confident in your salvation?

First, repent of all sin, quit practicing habitual sin, submit yourselves to God, and be obedient to all His commands. The Spirit of God gives you this formidable weapon of an offensive and defensive nature. The Word of God, the Scriptures, and truth according to His Word can be wielded with great results against your enemy. But, one has to read, study, and ingest the Word of God in order to use this sword of the Spirit. Pray in the Spirit in every situation. Use every kind of prayer and request there is. For the same reason, be alert. Use every kind of effort and make every kind of request for all of God's people (Ephesians 6:10-18, GWT).

Prayer is part of the armor of God. Once dressed in spiritual armor, you need the proper attitude, mindset, or worldview. Prayer to God is the proper mindset to keep you standing in the battle. When your emotions are being twisted and turned by your enemy, when fear is gripping you, and when you and your spouse are buried in confusion, then pray.

Pray for relief, pray for power and strength, pray for wisdom and revelation. Just keep praying. Be alert and exert yourself to win, to overcome in God's grace. The Apostle Peter wrote about alertness and clarity of mind. He knew that Satan attacks viciously through our thoughts and through our mental processes. One of the tests we developed to ascertain whether our emotions or thoughts were from a natural or demonic source was to determine the origin of the thought.

If for example, we were feeling sad or "weepy" and there was no mental activity precipitating it, then we knew it was of demonic origins. Likewise, if we were feeling angry or agitated and we could trace the emotion to some mental thought or event, then we knew it was natural. However, Satan can and, will use a "natural" emotion to get you into a wrong and negative mindset. In all reality, everything is spiritual. "Natural" is simply the evidence of the "supernatural." It is the outcome of the unseen world. Once again, everything is spiritual.

The Apostle Peter was well aware of Satan's ability to infiltrate the mind and that is why he wrote the church to keep their mind clear, and be alert. "Your opponent the devil is prowling around like a roaring lion as he looks for someone to devour. Be firm in the faith and resist him, knowing that other believers throughout the world are going through the same kind of suffering. God, who shows you his kindness and who has called you through Christ Jesus to his eternal glory, will restore you, strengthen you, make you strong, and support you as you suffer for a little while. Power belongs to him forever," (1Peter 5:8-11).

Do yourself a favor and reread the above Scripture. Now, read it again. Read it once again. It speaks for itself and says it all very clearly and succinctly. Listen to the exhortation, "Keep your mind clear and be alert." Do not allow your thoughts to wander down dark roads of guilt, shame, anger, hatred, lust, greed, or any other ungodly thought. Control your mind or Satan will.

The Nature of Faith

We wrote about having "faith" before, but now we want to really break it down for you. You must realize how important having faith in God is in combating the enemy of your marriage. In Ephesians 6:16, we read about the "shield of faith" for defeating the enemy's deadly barrage of sharp and hot arrows, which he shoots at you continually. Now, lets examine why faith or belief in God and His power to work miracles in your marriage is so important. Actually, it is so important that without faith, you may as well put down this book and give up. You need not go any further in fighting for the life of your marriage without faith or trust in God and His provision.

The writer of Hebrews gives us the definition of faith. Faith is the substance of things hoped for, faith is the belief and the confident assurance that the deed, the object, or the matter will happen, take place, or be obtained. It will occur. To "hope" for these things is to expect them to happen. To "hope" for these things is to confidently trust that they will materialize.

We must believe that it is possible. We must have belief in God's creative power. This is the beginning to a new spiritual life. God wants to take you and your marriage to new heights, challenges, and joys. You must exercise your faith in Him. It is impossible to gain any spiritual insight without faith.

When examining faith as it relates to spiritual warfare, we know that there are two sides of faith, the passive and the active side. The passive side is "submitting" to God's control and authority over our lives. It is passive in the sense that we are not actively battling with Satan, but are passively and humbly being dependent on God for all our needs (yet, this too is really part of warfare).

The active part of faith – when we get active in battle – comes when we "resist" Satan and his schemes. Understand that the "resisting" is futile without the "submitting." James 4:7, 8 (NKJV) states, "Therefore submit to God. Resist the devil and he will flee from you. Draw near to God and He will draw near to you. Cleanse your hands, you sinners; and purify your hearts, you double-minded."

The Source of Power

Now think about this. We, as believers, have the authority of Jesus Christ over Satan. Yes, Jesus has given us all authority regarding spiritual warfare. Once you really know this fact and know that it is Scriptural, it will liberate you from the fear and bondage of Satan. His scare and fear tactics will minimize and he will not be able or allowed to torment you and your marriage. You and your family can take authority over him. You can bind him and remove him from your body, house, family, and marriage.

This is an incredible revelation of God's power, and Satan does not want you to study these Scriptures, or to know about your authority. He does not want you to know this fact, really know it in your heart. See, he does not want to be arrested. He does not want to have to obey God's law. He does not want to be removed from tormenting you. Nonetheless, he has to leave in the name and power of our Lord Jesus Christ.

The closer you get to God, and the more you practice prayer and Scripture, the more power you will have. Satan will continue to attack you and attempt to bind you, however you will have the power and knowledge to resist him and defeat him in every battle. These are the Words from Jesus (God's Word Today) regarding this delegation. First, we must know that He has all authority over Satan. Jesus said regarding this fact, "All authority in heaven and on earth has been given to me," (Matthew 28:18). Second, we must know that He has delegated that authority to us.

After sending out 70 disciples to minister, they came back very happy. They said, "Lord, even demons obey us when we use the power and authority of your name!" Jesus said to them, "I watched Satan fall from heaven like lightning. I have given you the authority to trample snakes and scorpions and to destroy the enemy's power. Nothing will hurt you," (Luke 10:19).   Read and understand verse 19. Jesus has given His believers authority to be victorious, and to destroy Satan's power.

The Apostle John also wrote about Christ destroying Satan's works. The person who lives a sinful life belongs to the devil, because the devil has been committing sin since the beginning. The reason that the Son of God appeared was to destroy what the devil does (1John 3:8). Jesus also said that we would be destroying Satan's works through His authority. "I can guarantee this truth: Those who believe in Me will do the things that I am doing. They will do even greater things because I am going to the Father," (John 14:12).

Because Jesus knew God's plan for mankind's salvation, He said we would do great things because He would ascend into Heaven and be seated on the right side of God the Father, and we would be with Him in that position. He would give us His authority. Remember that we are in Christ and he in us. He is the head of the church and we are His body. We sit with Christ on God's right side in Heaven. Paul the Apostle wrote, "God has brought us back to life together with Christ Jesus and has given us a position in Heaven with him," (Ephesians 2:6).

Another portion of the Scripture tells about Christ's position. He is far above all rulers, authorities, powers, lords, and all other names that can be named, not only in this present world but also in the world to come. God has put everything under the control of Christ. He has made Christ the head of everything for the good of the church. The church is Christ's body and completes him as he fills everything in every way (Ephesians 1:21). Once again, the Scriptures tell us that we are Christ's body and are one with Him.

For example, the body is one unit and yet has many parts. As all the parts form one body, so it is with Christ. By one Spirit, we were all baptized into one body. Whether we are Jew or gentile, slave or free, God gave all of us one Spirit to drink (1Corinthians 12:13). We are the church, and we are Christ's body and so we share in His authority over rulers, powers, and all other evil kingdoms. We are one with the Spirit of Jesus.

The person who unites himself with the Lord becomes one spirit with Him, (1Corinthians 6:17). Paul declared about God, "He stripped the rulers and authorities of their power and made a public spectacle of them as He celebrated His victory in Christ," (Colossians 2:15). So, are you totally convinced that Christ has delegated His authority over the evil spirits to us?

You need to be certain that you will also know the unlimited greatness of His power as it works with might and strength for us, the believers. He worked with that same power in Christ when He brought him back to life and gave Him the highest position in heaven. You see, Christ's work on this earth is done, and we are His "body" to carry out His will here. He is the head, and the head needs a body to function. As His body, we have Christ as our head and all of His authority over evil, so that we can live bondage-free lives through Christ Jesus our Lord!

The Apostle Paul wrote, "Thank God that he gives us the victory through our Lord Jesus Christ," (1Corinthians 15:57). How do we have victory? God has rescued us from the power of darkness and has brought us into the kingdom of His Son, whom He loves. His Son paid the price to free us, which means that our sins are forgiven. He is the image of the invisible God, the firstborn of all creation. He created all things in heaven and on earth, visible and invisible.

Whether they are kings or lords, rulers or powers—everything has been created through Him and for Him.

War of the Mind

We have to guard our minds. Jesus has done his redemptive work on the cross and in the resurrection, and gave us His Spirit to guide us toward holiness. However, we have to exert our will toward "pressing" forward and onward toward obtaining the character of Christ. The Scriptures state that the weapons of our warfare are spiritual and used to bring down Satan's strongholds. These spiritual weapons are used for, "Casting down arguments and every high thing that exalts itself against the knowledge of God, *bringing every thought into captivity* to the obedience of Christ," (2Corintians 10:5, NIV, emphasis mine).

Notice the Scripture does not say that Jesus or the Holy Spirit will capture every "thought," it says we will do this with spiritual weapons. Guarding or policing the mind and/or heart is Scriptural. In Genesis, we read of two brothers who brought offerings to God with one offering being acceptable and the other unacceptable. The brother whose offering was unacceptable to God became angry, and allowed evil thoughts into his mind. The brother, called Cain, did not guard or police his mind, and this led to murder. God spoke to Cain, "Why this tantrum? Why the sulking?"

You can see in this passage the emotions starting to take control of Cain, emotions that form in the mind and in the thoughts. "If you do well, won't you be accepted?

252

And if you do not do well, sin is lying in wait for you, ready to pounce; it's out to get you, you've got to master it." God is telling Cain, just as He tells us today, that we must master our thoughts that lead to sin.

Cain had words with his brother Abel. They were out in the field; Cain attacked his brother and killed him, (Genesis 4:6-8, TMSG). Here is the sad result of thoughts and emotions run wild. Cain became a murderer and suffered great consequences for his sin. This was the direct result of failure to police the mind. Jesus taught about guarding the mind. He clearly stated that evil and sinful thoughts are akin to performing the actual act.

In Matthew 5:27, 28, He talks about lustful thoughts in the mind. "Do not go to bed with another's spouse. But, do not think you have preserved your virtue simply by staying out of bed. Your heart can be corrupted by lust even quicker than your body. Those leering looks you think nobody notices, they also corrupt you."

The Apostle Paul in Romans 12:2, discusses the need for us to continually police our thoughts. He warns us to not to become so well adjusted to our culture that we fit into it without even thinking. Instead, he admonishes, fix your attention on God, and you will change from the inside out. Readily recognize what He wants from you, and quickly respond to it. Unlike the culture around you, always dragging you down to its level of immaturity, God brings the best out of you, develops well-formed maturity in you.

So, is it enough to merely "not think bad thoughts" and gently swipe them away? No. We, as Christ followers must attack the evil thought with passion and with zeal. It is not enough to "block" the punch coming straight for our heads. We must "parry" the attack striking it down hard. Then after clearing the punch (the thought), we counter-attack with the Word of God, striking, slashing, cutting, and destroying the enemy's attack on us.

Strengthen the Covenant

In Malachi chapter two, a "call to faithfulness" for God's people occurs, and directly addresses the marriage covenant. Judah has cheated on God, a sickening violation of trust in Israel and Jerusalem: Judah has desecrated the holiness of God by falling in love and running off with foreign women, women who worship alien gods. God's curse is on those who do this! He commands to drive them out of house and home! They are no longer fit to be part of the community no matter how many offerings they bring to God.

There is a second offense to God. He says, "You fill the place of worship with your whining and sniveling because you do not get what you want from God. Do you know why? Simple. Because God was there as a witness when you spoke your marriage vows to your young bride, and now you have broken those vows, broken the faith-bond with your vowed companion, your covenant wife. God, not you, made marriage. His Spirit inhabits even the smallest details of marriage.

What does he want from marriage? Children of God, that is what. Therefore, guard the spirit of marriage within you. Do not cheat on your spouse. 'I hate divorce,' says the God of Israel. God-of-the-Angel-Armies says, 'I hate the violent dismembering of the one flesh of marriage.' So, watch yourselves. Do not let your guard down. Do not cheat," (Malachi 2:13-16, TMSG).

Ouch! If you love your God, you will heed this warning and stern rebuke. God cannot bless you, if you are cheating on your spouse. Christ said that the law forbade adultery, but even lusting after another person is the same as committing this sin. Just thinking about it and fantasizing over a make believe lover is like actually performing the act of adultery in the eyes of God. Men, you cannot fantasize over pornography (no matter what the delivery system is) and live a life pleasing to God. Ladies, you cannot fantasize over romance novels and chick-flicks, and please God in holiness with your mental adultery or fornication.

You may question if this act is bad, or if this act is wrong, but it is fornication (immorality) in the mind. If you have sexual fantasies about another person, real or make-believe, it is sin regardless of the act. If this is you, then you must ask for God's forgiveness, repent from your adultery, and start living for God. Nothing less will do and nothing less will protect you from the curse you have brought on yourself. God inhabits the smallest details in your marriage

Often, marriage is compared to the Kingdom of Heaven as it relates to Christ as the bridegroom and we, His bride. Marriage is not just an "agreement" or an "arrangement," but rather, a COVENANT. Much like the faithful covenant God makes with us, our marriage is a microcosm of that mystery. As God is faithful to us, we must replicate that faithfulness in our marriages. God wants spiritual children from us, as well as, godly, physical children. It is the responsibility of the parents to raise their children in the ways of God in order to perpetuate generational blessing and holiness.

Just as God's covenant with Abraham was designed to produce "children" that followed God, your marriage covenant is designed to produce both physical and spiritual children that know the LORD. If we pull from one another, it is like tearing apart one flesh. It is a bloody mess. So, honor your marriage and see it as God sees it.

The Prayer

How do you and your spouse walk with God, we mean really walk with God? It starts with the prayer or desire of your heart. You must ask God to come into your marriage and into your individual lives, and bring you closer to Him. As your marriage submits to the authority of the Almighty God, He will bring change and restoration into your relationship. The Holy Spirit will guide your marriage into all truth.

God has many names or authorities that your marriage can grasp and hold onto as pure truth. When the

Scripture reads that the Lord is your shepherd, and leads you, you can really hold onto that truth, knowing that it is superior to all surrounding circumstances or "realities" that could currently exist.

In the Gospel of Luke (11:1-4), Jesus instructs His disciples how to pray. Linda and I have found great comfort in praying God's Word back to Him, and in praying in the authority of the names of God. The following prayer can be used in the same way in your marriage.

Our Father in Heaven.

The Greek Word for father connotes respect, dignity, author and initiator of everything, and implicit faith in one as a child would have in its father. This is Jehovah Rohi, or God is my shepherd. When you pray to your Heavenly Father, approach Him in the name and authority of His character as the one who shepherds your marriage.

Hallowed be Your Name.

The Word "hallowed" is a Greek verb. That means it is an action word meaning to withdraw from fellowship with the world by first gaining fellowship with God, the Father. This is a name of God. It is Jehovah Mekkahdishkim, or the Lord who sanctifies me. So, it could be spoken as, "Sanctifying is your name," "Your name (faith in) makes me holy," or "Setting me apart is your name." When you pray, you are recognizing and believing that God is your shepherd leader who continually sets your life apart for His purpose.

Your kingdom come and your will be done on earth as it is in Heaven.

Jehovah Tsidkenu is the name of God that means, "God our Righteousness." Christ-followers must anticipate the day when all of God's defeated enemies are totally subdued and destroyed when all things are consummated. Only then, will the world be ruled in righteousness and justice. We pray that God's will is accomplished both on earth and in Heaven based on His righteousness.

Give us day by day our daily bread.

There are two names of God in this passage. First, there is Jehovah Jireh, or the God who provides. This is seen in the statement, "Give us day by day." Every day, we can expect God to provide for us. This is in Scripture. Christ told his followers not to worry about clothes, food, and other things of life because God knew what they needed (not wanted or coveted, but needed). When you pray with your spouse over your marriage, you can call on the name of God who provides your day-by-day needs, both physically and spiritually.

The second name of God contained in this statement is El Shaddai, or the all-sufficient sustaining God. The "daily bread" that is given to us is from the all supplying, all sufficient, and all sustaining God. He will give your marriage the "bread" that it must have to be sustained. God will supply the nutrients needed for your marriage to grow and flourish. You can confidently pray, knowing God will supply what your marriage needs, as well as, what it requires to be sustained.

Forgive us our sins; we also forgive everyone who is indebted to us.

El Shaddai is also the covenant name of God, which He gave to Abraham. He is the God who forgives, saves, and redeems. It is through His power that we Christ-followers are able to forgive others who have harmed us. As Christ-followers, we can be certain that all of our sins are forgiven, and that we are given the internal character to forgive others also. This applies to your spouse. Forgive one another, and ask God to forgive you for all your sins against Him.

And do not lead us into temptation, but deliver us from the evil one.

The Greek Word for temptation is used of a "trial," "testing," or "proving" for the purpose of discovering a strength or weakness in a person. The "testing" or discovery of evil can be for the person's own benefit. They are enlightened to their own shortcomings, which cause them to repent and change their behavior.

The Greek word for deliver is used to connote a drawing away with "force," "violence," or "to drag," or "pull out" of calamity or danger. It means essentially "to liberate." Evil one is translated from the Greek Word, "poneros." It means labor, sorrow, pain, or the weariness of it all. It means evil in a moral or spiritual sense. Also, it has the implication of mischief and malice.

259

Christ-followers can expect to "not be led" into a sin-discovery testing period based on their own submission to Satan's mischief. Rather, they can expect to be violently dragged away from Satan's malice so they do not succumb to sin, having then, to be led into a proving ground.

To be violently dragged away or pulled forcibly from danger often hurts. We as Christ-followers are asking God to violently remove us (even if it hurts) from Satan's mischief and malice so that we do not succumb to sin. Once we sin, God will have to bring it into the light by testing and trying our faith, so that we can repent and return walking with Him. This is what it means to ask God "not to lead us into a temptation or proving ground" by snatching us away (giving us the power to live holy lives) from Satan's deceit.

The God who delivers us from Satan is called Jehovah Nissi, or God is our banner. God is our victory over sin, evil, and Satan. We Christ-followers pray to "God our victory" to make us separate and holy so we do not succumb to Satan's lies and, commit sin. Therefore, we do not need to be corrected because of our willful sinful behavior. We are actually praying for the Holy Spirit to bring us into holiness. Holiness is our ultimate weapon against Satan's mischief and malice. Of all the methods discussed to defeat the enemy of your marriage, living a holy life to God is the ultimate and highest method.

This entire book hinges on the premise of holiness or sanctification. All of the methods, discussion, and techniques are encompassed in the idea of holiness.

This is what a true Marital Marriage looks like. If you and your spouse desire to be Christ-like, take on the very nature of Christ, and are willing to be led by the Holy Spirit, then holiness is the life you chose. And Satan is defeated by a holy lifestyle. His power is nullified by a holy marriage.

Is it easy to deny yourself, take up your cross, and follow Jesus? The path leading to eternal life is narrow, so count the cost. But, what good is it if you gain the whole world, but then lose your soul? So, "Christ-like-ness" is the real goal. Many people call themselves "Christians," and are on their way to Hell. Few really show the character, love, and suffering of Jesus.

Satan is defeated through Jesus Christ. That is why we must be like Him. We are in a "mop up" operation militarily speaking. Our enemies are defeated, but we as the soldiers of the reigning Kingdom are mopping up and waiting for the end of time and history. Meanwhile, our foes, knowing that their time is short, continue to engage us in skirmishes and warfare. They resist their destruction.

The whole idea is to become the "ideal man" or to become Christ-like. The entire goal of sanctification is to become holy like God is holy. It is the renewing of the mind. It is the circumcising of the heart. It is becoming a person full of faith and full of God's Spirit. This entire book is written on that principle.

This is the only way to defeat the enemy of your marriage. Anything less is futile. You may or may not

261

have demons in your marriage bed; however, this Christian life is war, and fought spiritually, not physically or naturally. This is spiritual warfare. This is the path in obtaining a Martial Marriage.

We must, we have to – die to self. The person that we are, that carnal, natural person has to be crucified daily in order that the Spirit of Christ can become more alive in us. This is the ultimate weapon against Satan. We are reborn in Christ, little babies and little infants. But, we grow into mature Christian adults through experience, both good and bad. Do not criticize your spouse, or blame them for their shortcomings. Pray for one another, uphold each other in the presence of God, and collectively commit to serving the Lord with all of your being.

Do not allow the enemy of your marriage to rob you. Do not sleep while he steals your peace. Do not hesitate when he tries to crush you under destruction. There is so much more to our existence. There are eternal things and treasures. There are kingdoms to be judged and wars to be fought. These are exciting times in the Spirit. However, only through the revelation of the Holy Spirit, will we ever get to the place of appreciation for godly things.

We pray for God's grace, mercy, and peace for your marriage. God is always merciful and He is always full of grace, but peace only comes from abiding in Him. Often, it only comes after a violent brutal war. Get your scars. Fight hard.

Chapter 13: Self-Deliverance From Fear Demons

The spirit of fear often comes in through rejection and acts like a strongman in a person allowing other spirits to enter and torment. We have learned that once the spirit of fear is removed, many other torments leave as well. Some of fear's cohorts are self-awareness, fear of man, fear of disapproval, sensitivity, anxiety, dread, apprehension, and a host of other manifestations.

Pray that the Holy Spirit brings to your mind the names of the spirits that have to go. You have the authority, as a believer in Jesus Christ, to self-expel the spirit of fear and everything else that may be attached to you. Remember, deliverance is an ongoing process, and things start coming off you as the Holy Spirits readies you. What we are going to do is get that process started by backing the spirit of fear off and away from you.

Your Authority in Yeshua

The Gospel of Mark 16:17 and 18 commands, "And these signs shall follow them that believe; in my name shall they cast out devils, they shall speak with new tongues; they shall take up serpents; and if they drink any deadly thing, it shall not hurt them; they shall lay hands on the sick, and they shall recover."

These are miracles that follow "faithers" in Christ. Notice that in the Gospel of Mark "devils" are associated with physical and mental sickness. The taking up of demonic serpents and ingesting demonic sorcery will not harm us if we are under the blood of our LORD, doing His will. We speak in a new language of Christ, following His example. We shall lay hands on the sick and they shall recover. Debilitating fear is a sickness caused by demons, and they have to go in the name of Yeshua of Nazareth.

In other words, we command the spirit of fear to release its grip on your mind and drive it out in the name of Yeshua. Demons are disembodied spirits that attach, oppress, vex, and harass all people, even good Christians. It is our responsibility to take our God given authority over them and drive them away from us and from others.

In Luke 10:19, Jesus commands, "Behold, I give **YOU** the authority to trample on serpents and scorpions, and over all the power of the enemy, and **NOTHING** shall by any means hurt **YOU**." This authority is for us just as much as it was for His early disciples. We want you to take authority over the things that are causing you pain and suffering. Read the prayer below, believing with all faith in the all mighty power of God to deliver you from the spirit of fear using the God given authority you have through the blood and redemption of our LORD Yeshua our Savior.

But first, make sure that you have confessed all sin to your savior and that you have forgiven anyone that you may hold a grudge against. This is important because non-forgiveness will hinder deliverance, and may even give demonic spirits a legal right to torment a person. Ask yourself if you have any such non-forgiveness, hatred, or animosity toward anyone. Forgiving is a matter of "will" and not of "emotion." You can "will" to forgive, even if you do not "feel" like it. Willingly forgive and let go of anything that may hinder your healing. This is highly important.

Now, you have legal authority over demons and spiritual authority to expel them from your mind and body. The enemy or sickness has no right to take what belongs to you because you belong to God! Amen! We are in agreement with you. "If two or more agree on anything touching this world, in my name, it shall be done."

Deliverance Prayer

"Dear heavenly Father, we come to You through the redemption and shed blood of our LORD Yeshua, our savior and healer, and redeemer. It is through His authority, which He commissioned to us through His Word that we now come and do battle against the powers of the enemy that would make us sick. We put the devils, spirits, serpents, and scorpions on notice right now that in the holy name of Yeshua our LORD that they must obey the commands of God and release and go! Go! Go in the name of Yeshua of Nazareth, in the name of Yeshua Go!

In the name of Yeshua, we bind the work of the enemy right now, and we bind it and prevent the spirit of fear from strengthening itself. We break every demonic attachment and stronghold on mind, body, and soul.

Spirit of fear, fear of man, low self esteem, fear of disapproval, fear of judgment, fear of condemnation, and sensitiveness, we command you right now in the authority of Yeshua our LORD to go! You go in the name of Yeshua of Nazareth.

We command healing to enter into the body and heal the damage caused by the enemy, who tried to steal, kill, and destroy. We cancel that assignment right now! Dear LORD, we ask for Your Holy Spirit to fill the void left by this evil spirit and bring PEACE, trust, faith, and wholeness in Yeshua our LORD. We thank You Father for all these things, in the holy and mighty name of Yeshua of Nazareth, amen."

Follow Through

Do not allow Satan to tell you this is weird or strange. Do not allow anyone to tell you that you must accept this fear. Satan will try to steal the seed. Be aware of that. If you want to see that this is totally Biblical, then read the Gospel of Mark and notice that most of Jesus' ministry was healing the sick (children of God of Israel) by the removing of demonic spirits that caused the sickness. Enough of the weak willed faithless religion so many subscribe to, it is time to get mean and command these things to go from you, in the authority of Yeshua our LORD.

Keeping your deliverance is the next step. We know this is quite a bit of information, so we will keep this section short and to the point.

1. Whenever you feel attacked or feel the spirit of fear creeping up on you, apply the blood of Yeshua to your mind, soul, and body, submit to God and the enemy will have to flee (Revelation 12:10; James 4:7).

2. Put on the whole armor of God (Ephesians 6:10-18).

3. Stay in the Word of God (read and study) and renew your thoughts with God's thoughts (Psalms 119:105; Romans 12:2).

4. Practice prayer, praise, and thanksgiving (Philippians 4:6; Colossians 4:2).

5. DWELL in the secret place of the most high, which means to cultivate your relationship with God, and ABIDE under the shadow of the Almighty, which is walking in obedience to what he teaches you in His word (Psalm 91:1; John 15:5). This is the key to staying demon free.

6. Example One: When the enemy comes at you with the spirit of fear, submit to God, then take authority over that spirit, and tell it to leave you in the name of the Lord Yeshua of Nazareth (James 4:7; Luke 10:19).

7. Example Two: When the enemy attacks your mind, submit to God, cast down the imagination, and then replace it with the truth of God's word (2 Corinthians 10:5; Romans 12:2).

Remember, We can do all things through Christ, which strengthens us.

Ministry Information

KAPOW Radio Show Network

In November 2011, when we published the original eBook edition of "Demons in My Marriage Bed," we had just begun to experiment with an Internet radio show. It is "radio" in the sense that we can conduct live shows, take callers, and run a chat room. It is a "podcast" because all of the shows are archived and can be heard at the listener's convenience.

We needed a name for our show that reflected our passion for teaching others about spiritual warfare and Biblical truths. Linda came up with the name "KAPOW," which stands for Kingdom Against Powers Of Wickedness! A better name did not exist. So, we were off and running and conducted our first show in late October 2011 with one listener, and that was Paul's sister!

However, God kept giving us lessons to teach and words to speak and the show grew, and is still growing in the grace and power of our LORD Yeshua. Three years later in late 2014, we average 8,000 to 10,000 listeners every 30 days. KAPOW Radio Show has now become a network where we conduct two shows a week and have other like-minded hosts conducting shows for the remaining days. The network provides solid Bible based teaching and discussions throughout the week and listeners can access the content at any time that is convenient for them.

www.kapowradioshow.com

The above website contains all of the information you need to access the shows on the network in addition to containing a radio player on the site. KAPOW Radio Show Network can be downloaded as an iTunes podcast and has its own Apple and Android apps for easy listening. The Network uses both Blog Talk Radio and Spreaker Radio for broadcasting platforms. The KAPOW Radio Show website also contains information about episode schedules with biographies of the network hosts.

The KAPOW Radio Show is produced and sponsored by Fifthook Media, an online digital publisher of eBooks, music, and radio programming. Fifthook Media pays the cost to produce all episodes, and everything is **FREE** to the listener. KAPOW Radio show does NOT accept monetary donations from anyone. You will never see a "donate" button on the KAPOW or Fifthook Media websites.

In 2010, we wanted to form our own small publishing business so we could write, produce, and publish our own books for distribution to readers. Linda formulated the name from the term "Fighting For The Heart Of Our King," and thus Fifthook Media was born. Please visit Fifthook Media's website to see our other books about spiritual warfare and Christian living. Additionally, there are many FREE resources on the site as well including free music, free eBooks, and free teaching categorized for your convenience.

Of course, the KAPOW Radio Show can be accessed from this site, and links to the two apps and podcast subscription are there as well. We invite you to explore our site and take advantage of the many resources on there, which will contribute positively to your spiritual growth.

www.facebook.com/fifthookmedia

Join Fifthook Media on face book. This page posts the most recent bizarre, demonic, and alternative news that you can find in order to stimulate discussion about the evil and perilous times in which we live. Our face book page is dedicated to exposing and warning against the powers of wickedness and evil pervading our planet.

Linda Villanueva earned degrees in Mathematics, Science and Behavioral Science. She earned a Bachelor of Science Degree in Nutrition and Dietetics from Loma Linda University in California. She has over 25-years in administrative employment with both federal and local governments. Her passion for intercessory prayer and Biblical hermeneutics has enhanced her interest in spiritual warfare. She is the co-author of "Demons in My Marriage Bed: A True Story of Spiritual Warfare," "Eyes to See Unseen Enemies," "Idol'-i-cide: The Killing of Idols," and "Christianity of Blasphemy: A New Gnostic Lie."

Paul Villanueva earned a Bachelor of Arts degree in Biblical Studies and Systematic Theology from Southeastern University in Florida. He received a Master of Arts degree in Negotiation and Conflict Management from California State University Dominguez Hills. He has over 25-years in law enforcement and obtained to the rank of Police Lieutenant. Paul authored "The Wisdom of Death: Six Paths to Understanding Loss and Grief," and "Martial Arts: A Biblical Perspective." He is the co-author of "Demons in My Marriage Bed: A True Story of Spiritual Warfare," "Eyes to See Unseen Enemies," "Idol'-i-cide: The Killing of Idols," and "Christianity of Blasphemy: A New Gnostic Lie."

More Books by The Authors

"Eyes to See Unseen Enemies"

Eyes to See Unseen Enemies," is a polemic or argument against the cultural "little c-Christianity" of today, which is a false religion serving a false god with a pseudo Christ. This breakthrough work assists the reader in understanding the massive error occurring in the contemporary "post-modern-neo-pagan church" due to its lack of Biblical teaching and behavior. With the church's emerging psychology, entertainment, marketing, mysticism, and occultism, cultural Christianity is on the path of judgment. Those who refuse to heed the warnings and spurn leaving the false worship of cultural Christianity will perish with it.

The reader will receive insight about the severity of the cultural church's condition. Insight from the author's knowledge of Biblical truths, their personal dreams along with some frightening prophetic visions regarding the false reality of a religion that has a form of godliness, but lacks the power of the true creator God to fully transform lives and save souls from destruction. This book will cement the differences between neo-pagan worship occurring in many Christian organizations, comparing them to the true Biblical "Ecclesia (called-out-ones)," or better known as the real Bride of Christ.

Challenging and informative, it will leave the hearer and seer of Biblical truth with a vital decision to make, which will determine whether or not he or she will leave the Babylonian false religion of cultural Christianity, or suffer in its punishment from the wrath of God. Judgment begins at the house of God, and this work is an urgent message for an urgent time.

"Idol-i-cide: The Killing of Idols"

What is idolicide? It is a word we invented to refer to the killing of idols. Idolicide is a noun, but we use it with the intent of an action verb. We want the reader to take action against the idols, which prevent a true worship of the All Mighty God in spirit and in truth, and we want the reader to destroy those idols from their lives. God has commanded, "You shall have no other gods before me." It is that simple. The command and the requirement never changed, and we all must actively seek out those idolatrous things in our lives that would prevent us from having eternal life and salvation with our Father God.

Pagan gods and goddesses are easily recognized, but what about the subtle idols of attitude, behavior, or belief systems? Anything that stands in the way between you and the All Mighty God is an idol. Together we will explore and expose the hidden idols of tradition, religion, doubt, impatience, false worship, self-pity, and much more. Together we will commit idolicide and gain new perspectives and deliverance from demonic strongholds. This book is about spiritual warfare. It is the beginning of battle preparation, and is foundational in living a victorious and overcoming life.

"Martial Arts: A Biblical Perspective"

A 6,000 word well researched mini book on the compatibility between the Martial Arts and Christianity. This work explores the history of ancient fighting arts, the philosophies rooted in the fighting systems, the differences between traditional and non-traditional fighting schools, fitness and heath, Mixed Martial Arts or MMA, the dangers of yogic meditation, and the Biblical viewpoint concerning such practices. It will enlighten your understanding and give you confidence in a decision to practice or not to practice these ancient fighting arts.

This is a must read for any Christian parent having a child enrolled in any type of fighting art school. It presents a fair and balanced viewpoint supported by documentation and Scriptural references. Many Martial arts experts were consulted and their views are outlined in a factual manner.

Author, Paul Villanueva holds a second-degree black belt in the Martial Art of Kung Fu San Soo. He has over twenty-five years of law enforcement experience, and was a California state certified instructor in Use of Force techniques for police officers.

He is also a Tactical Communications (Verbal Judo) expert and has appeared on a California state training DVD distributed to every police department in the state. Villanueva earned a Bachelor of Arts degree in Biblical Studies and a Master of Arts degree in Negotiation and Conflict Management.

"The Wisdom of Death: Six Paths to Understanding Loss and Grief"

The greatest fault found in other grief and loss books is they have not "systemized" the understanding process. Popular works have the information the reader needs so desperately spread throughout their pages or contained in multiple books.

There was a need for a book that plainly and simply "systemized" the journey through death, grief, sorrow, and anger. Needed was a book, which took the wisdom of the ages and applied it to several simple steps or paths.

The Wisdom of Death: Six Paths to Understanding Loss and Grief fills that need. It gathers the most important aspects of understanding loss and places them in a six-path system that enables the griever to grasp universal wisdom and truth easily and orderly.

Especially helpful is a "death timeline" where one can approximately determine a loved one's death by observing certain physical and spiritual symptoms. Also, the author discusses methods to responding to others, who are mourning, through a natural empathy. This is called the A.I.M. approach and has assisted many people.

The book contains information in an appendix that discusses financial matters one may face after losing a loved one. This includes a very useful and practical financial checklist. Cons, scams and other financial pitfalls are also examined.

Packed with wisdom, practical advice, and a spiritual view, The Wisdom of Death is a must read book for anyone who has lost a loved one through death. This book was born from first hand experience with the dying process rather than from a cold clinical psychological perspective. The author experienced everything he writes about.

The Wisdom of Death will impart to the reader a better understanding of the dying and grieving process.

###